Canon EOS R5 Mark II
User Guide

Master Every Button, Video Mode, and Autofocus Setting with Real-World Walkthroughs, Pro Tips, and Hands-On Guidance for Photographers & Filmmakers

Randy Osborn

Copyright © 2025 by Randy Osborn

Disclaimer:

This book is an independent publication and is not affiliated with, authorized by, sponsored by, or endorsed by Canon Inc. or any of its subsidiaries. Canon®, EOS®, and any related model names, logos, and branding are trademarks or registered trademarks of Canon Inc., which are used solely for descriptive and educational purposes.

All product names, logos, and brands mentioned in this book are the property of their respective owners. The information contained in this guide is based on publicly available resources, personal experience, research, and practical testing. It is intended for educational and informational purposes only and should not be considered official Canon documentation.

While every effort has been made to ensure the accuracy and usefulness of the content, the author and publisher make no warranties or representations regarding the completeness, reliability, or applicability of the techniques, settings, or recommendations presented. The use of any camera gear or shooting method is solely at the reader's discretion and risk.

Always consult the official Canon user manual or authorized Canon support for up-to-date product specifications, firmware changes, and warranty-related concerns.

By reading this book, you acknowledge that the author and publisher shall not be held liable for any loss, damage, or injury resulting from the use or misuse of the information provided.

Table of Contents

Meet the Beast — Canon EOS R5 Mark II Overview

Preface

Unlock the full power of your Canon EOS R5 Mark II with this *all-in-one, beginner-friendly guide*—meticulously crafted for photographers, filmmakers, content creators, and YouTubers who want *professional results without the guesswork*. Whether you're switching from Sony, upgrading from DSLR, or stepping into mirrorless full-frame cameras for the first time, this book walks you through *step-by-step mastery* of every setting, mode, and creative tool your Canon R5 Mark II has to offer.

This Canon EOS R5 Mark II user guide 2025 is the perfect resource to help you feel confident with every button press. From Canon R5 Mark II photography tips to clean HDMI setup, autofocus video settings, Canon Log 3 color grading, and 8K/4K HQ video recording, you'll gain a real-world understanding of what works, what doesn't, and how to *maximize your gear* from day one.

Inside this Canon EOS R5 II camera book guide, you'll learn:

- Canon R5 camera setup step-by-step: From unboxing to shooting in full manual, we guide you through an *easy Canon R5 setup guide* with intuitive menu walkthroughs and customization tips
- Canon R5 autofocus tutorial: Learn how to choose the *best autofocus mode for Canon R5*, understand *eye detection autofocus*, fix common issues like *autofocus not working*

Canon R5, and take full advantage of *Dual Pixel AF II explained*

- Video mastery simplified: Master *Canon R5 video setup, Canon R5 II slow motion settings, Canon R5 video frame rates, Canon R5 10-bit H.265*, and understand *Canon R5 II video mode explained*—whether you're filming weddings, vlogging, or producing *YouTube-ready, studio-quality* content

- Overheating and performance: Practical *Canon EOS R5 Mark II overheating fix* strategies, *Canon R5 overheating solution* tips, and how to prevent issues like *Canon R5 battery drains fast*, or *Canon R5 not recording to card*

- Advanced features made simple: A deep dive into *Canon Log 3 and 10-bit video guide, Canon R5 C-Log color grading, Canon R5 white balance tips*, and *Canon R5 shutter speed guide* so you can shoot in any condition with cinematic precision

- Customization & workflow: Customize buttons, set up *Custom Modes C1, C2, C3*, and create *real-world setups* for travel, studio, and run-and-gun scenarios

- Memory cards & storage: Learn which cards work best with your camera: *CFexpress vs SD card Canon*, especially for 8K video, and *which card to use for 8K Canon* without fail

- Lens and accessories: Discover the *best lenses for Canon EOS R5 Mark II* for every genre—*wildlife, portrait, wedding, filmmaking*, and more

- Canon R5 Mark II for creators: *Creator-friendly*, *fast learning curve*, with sections tailored *for YouTubers*, *for vloggers*, *for Canon switchers*, and anyone seeking *confident shooting*

Also included:

- Fix blurry Canon R5 photos
- How to stop Canon R5 wobble
- Canon R5 clean HDMI output
- Canon R5 HDMI live streaming
- Canon R5 menu walkthrough
- Canon R5 wedding settings
- Preferred Canon R5 settings for video
- Canon R5 Mark II tutorial for beginners
- Canon R5 vs Sony A7RV comparison
- What is Canon Log 3 used for?
- Canon mirrorless full-frame camera guide

Whether you're capturing epic landscapes, shooting wildlife, recording weddings, or building a content empire, this Canon R5 Mark II manual for beginners will equip you with everything you need to shoot like a pro—fast. Say goodbye to frustration and hello to *step-by-step mastery*.

No more guesswork. No more missed shots. Just results.

Your journey to becoming a confident R5 Mark II shooter starts here.

Introduction

Who This Book Is For

This book was written for four distinct types of creators—and if you're holding it, chances are you're one of them.

1. Beginners who feel overwhelmed.

Maybe this is your first professional-grade mirrorless camera. You opened the box, saw the menus, the modes, the acronyms, and thought: *"Where do I even start?"* You're not alone. The Canon EOS R5 Mark II is a powerful machine, but without guidance, it can feel like stepping into the cockpit of a fighter jet without a pilot's license. This book will gently walk you through each function—button by button, screen by screen—so you can take full control of your gear with confidence, even if you're brand new to the Canon ecosystem or photography in general.

2. Enthusiasts who want to unlock every feature.

Maybe you've shot with DSLRs, maybe you're upgrading from the original R5, or maybe you're transitioning from another brand. You've got a good handle on aperture, ISO, and autofocus—but you're hungry to master 8K RAW, custom modes, Canon Log 3, or subject tracking across multiple zones. This guide goes beyond surface-level tutorials and gives you real-world workflows and breakdowns of the most powerful (but often hidden) features of the R5 Mark II.

3. Professionals who need speed and reliability.

You don't have time to sift through a 500-page manual or dig through forums when you're on a paid shoot. You need a reference that cuts through the noise and gives you efficient, tested setups for portraits, wildlife, weddings, commercial, and video gigs. Whether you shoot for clients, agencies, or yourself, this guide includes pro-level configurations, lens pairing advice, and troubleshooting tips to keep your workflow smooth and reliable under pressure.

4. Content creators and filmmakers who want cinema-level results.

This camera wasn't just built for stills—it's a full-blown video powerhouse. But if you've ever wondered *how to shoot cinematic 4K or 8K footage, how to color grade Canon Log, or how to avoid overheating during a live shoot*, you're in the right place. We'll help you design a creator's rig that maximizes your results—whether you're vlogging, building a YouTube channel, capturing client interviews, or producing short films.

This book was built for anyone who wants to make *art* with the Canon EOS R5 Mark II—and avoid the trial and error that wastes time, ruins shots, or leaves you doubting your gear.

Why the Canon R5 Mark II Stands Out

The Canon EOS R5 Mark II isn't just an incremental upgrade—it's a next-generation creative machine that redefines what's possible in the mirrorless space. Canon listened to user feedback from the original R5 and delivered something that not only pushes boundaries but also solves problems that limited creators in the past.

Here's why it matters:

- **Image quality that rivals medium format**: With its high-resolution full-frame sensor, improved dynamic range, and remarkable color science, the R5 II produces images that are clean, crisp, and cinematic straight out of the camera.
- **Cinema-grade 8K and 4K video with better thermal control**: Unlike its predecessor, the R5 II offers longer recording times, internal 8K 60p RAW, **and** smart heat management, making it viable for serious filmmakers, not just occasional video shooters.
- **Deep Learning Autofocus with AI-powered tracking**: Eye, animal, bird, and even vehicle detection now run on advanced AI algorithms. The system predicts movement with uncanny accuracy—even in low light—making missed focus a thing of the past.
- **IBIS that works in harmony**: In-body stabilization has been refined to reduce that "wobble" effect when using wide

lenses—especially helpful for handheld video or run-and-gun shoots.

- **CFexpress + SD Dual Slots for flexible media workflows**: Whether you're shooting massive RAW sequences or need backup video capture, the dual card system offers speed and peace of mind.

This camera is Canon's answer to both Sony's cutting-edge tech and users' demands for a *hybrid workhorse*. It bridges photography and filmmaking in a way few cameras have. But with that power comes complexity—and that's where this guide comes in.

What This Guide Will Help You Achieve

By the end of this book, you won't just know how to *use* the Canon R5 Mark II—you'll know how to command it. You'll transform from an unsure operator into a confident visual storyteller who can:

- **Shoot confidently in manual mode**—knowing exactly how to set aperture, shutter speed, ISO, and white balance for any lighting scenario.
- **Customize your autofocus system** for every scenario: portrait sessions, wildlife tracking, kids in motion, low-light filming, and more.
- **Record cinematic video** with Canon Log 3, manage file types like H.265, and apply color grading techniques in your editing software with clarity and ease.

- **Avoid common frustrations** like overheating, memory card errors, IBIS/lens conflict, and battery drain—by knowing exactly what causes them and how to fix them.
- **Build your own perfect workflow**—with personalized button layouts, custom profiles, and "My Menu" settings that save you time on every shoot.
- **Capture moments that matter**—whether it's your child's first steps, a paying client's wedding, or your next viral YouTube short—with stunning clarity, depth, and emotion.

You'll stop fumbling through menus, second-guessing settings, or missing key moments. Instead, you'll shoot with precision, fluidity, and full creative control.

How to Use This Book (Interactive Style, Visuals, Scenarios, QR Bonus Access)

This is not a typical camera manual. It was written for real people doing real creative work. Every chapter is crafted with intention to guide you in a hands-on, practical, and visual way. Here's how to get the most from it:

- **Visual learning, not tech jargon**
  Expect annotated screenshots, lens comparison photos, button mapping illustrations, and before/after shooting

scenarios. We use imagery and plain English to explain what the Canon manual buries in cryptic codes.

- **Real-world scenarios > theoretical settings**
  You won't just learn *what* a setting does—you'll learn *when and why to use it*, based on actual genres and challenges: portraits, landscapes, events, YouTube videos, slow-motion shorts, and more.

- **Quick-start recipes at your fingertips**
  Need a fast setup for shooting pets indoors, or recording talking-head video in natural light? Each part of the book includes "Quick Setup Recipes" so you can skip the tech and just get the shot.

- **QR codes for bonus content**
  Some chapters include QR codes linking to exclusive downloadable resources:
  - Printable one-page cheat sheets
  - Sample video LUTs
  - Color grading guides
  - Bonus behind-the-scenes tutorials
  - Lens recommendation charts

- **Modular reading flow**
  You can read this book cover to cover, or jump straight to the part you need—whether that's autofocus setup, overheating fixes, or custom video profiles. Each chapter stands alone with cross-references to help you explore deeper.

This isn't just a book—it's your field guide, mentor, and secret weapon for turning the Canon R5 Mark II into an extension of your creative mind.

Welcome to the next level. Let's begin.

Part I: Essential Camera Setup & Controls

Chapter 1

Meet the Beast — Canon EOS R5 Mark II Overview

You're holding one of the most powerful creative tools ever made. The Canon EOS R5 Mark II is more than just an upgrade—it's a statement. A machine built to meet the evolving demands of photographers, filmmakers, and hybrid creators who expect excellence and refuse to compromise. But what makes this camera so special? Why is it already making waves across studios, wildlife reserves, wedding halls, and YouTube sets around the world?

Let's strip away the hype and jargon and look closely at what this beast truly offers—and why it might just be the best camera Canon has ever built.

What's New: Canon EOS R5 Mark II vs R5 and R5 C

To appreciate the R5 Mark II, it helps to understand where it came from. The original Canon EOS R5, released in 2020, was Canon's bold leap into the mirrorless battlefield. It stunned the market with

8K video, 45 megapixels, and next-gen autofocus, but it wasn't without flaws. Overheating issues, short video record times, and missing pro features left many creators waiting for a better balance.

Then came the Canon EOS R5 C, a hybrid of photo and cinema DNA, with a fan for extended video use—but it lost in-body stabilization and a few conveniences. It was powerful, but not seamless for those who shoot both photo and video regularly.

Now we have the Canon EOS R5 Mark II, which brings together the best of both previous models—and fixes what held them back. Here's how it stacks up:

Feature	Canon R5	Canon R5 C	Canon R5 Mark II
Sensor	45MP	45MP	45MP (improved processing)
Autofocus	Dual Pixel	Same	New AI deep

	CMOS AF II		learning with predictive
Video	8K/30p (RAW internal), limited record time	8K/60p (Cinema RAW Light) with active cooling	8K/60p RAW internal, longer recording, better thermals
Cooling	Passive, overheats quickly	Active cooling fan	Passive cooling with improved heat sink

IBIS	Yes	No	Yes, refined with gyro data for better stability
Log Profiles	Canon Log, Log 3	Canon Log, Log 2, Log 3	Canon Log 3, improved dynamic range
Weight	738g	770g	745g
Touchscreen	Vari-angle	Vari-angle	Vari-angle, faster response

Battery Life	Moderate	Longer	Improved with better efficiency

In short, the R5 Mark II is Canon's answer to three years of feedback. It keeps the photography prowess of the R5, incorporates the filmmaking finesse of the R5 C, and irons out the pain points that limited both.

Key Specs and Capabilities Explained in Plain English

The spec sheet is impressive, but what does it actually mean for *you*? Here's a breakdown in human language:

- **Sensor**:
  A 45-megapixel full-frame CMOS sensor means your photos will have incredible detail. You can crop in without losing quality, print billboard-sized images, or downscale for clean, noise-free web use.
- **Image Processor (DIGIC X Dual)**:
  This dual processor setup allows faster autofocus, better heat

management, and smoother file processing—whether you're capturing wildlife or shooting 8K video.

- **Video Formats**:

You can now record 8K RAW at 60fps internally—that's cinema-quality footage, captured straight to your card, with deep color data for grading. And yes, it handles long clips *without overheating* like its predecessor.

- **Canon Log 3 + 10-bit 4:2:2**:

For video creators, this means rich tonal range and color depth. You can shoot flat for post-production or vibrant for instant upload-ready footage.

- **Autofocus**:

The new AI-powered subject tracking recognizes eyes, faces, animals, birds, and vehicles. It predicts motion, locks on faster, and adapts in real time—even when your subject turns away or moves erratically.

- **IBIS (In-Body Image Stabilization)**:

Up to 8 stops of stabilization, meaning you can shoot handheld at low shutter speeds or walk while filming and still get buttery-smooth footage. It's also now smarter about when to defer to lens stabilization.

- **Viewfinder and LCD**:

A 5.76-million-dot OLED EVF and a fully articulating 3.2" LCD touchscreen give you crisp previews whether you shoot stills or video.

- **Dual Card Slots**:

CFexpress for heavy lifting (8K, burst mode), SD UHS-II

for flexibility. You can shoot to both simultaneously for backup or split stills/video.

- **Connectivity**:
Built-in Wi-Fi, Bluetooth, FTP, USB-C 3.2 for fast transfers, tethering, and even streaming or webcam use without additional gear.

- **Weather Sealing**:
Built to survive tough environments—dust, moisture, light rain, desert shoots, or on-location stress.

These aren't just specs—they're real tools that unlock what's possible in the field, studio, or on the road.

Understanding Mirrorless Mastery: What Makes It Different?

If you're coming from a DSLR like the 5D Mark IV or even the original EOS R, the shift to mirrorless may feel like a leap. Here's what you need to understand about how the R5 Mark II is designed to see and respond differently.

1. Full-Frame Mirrorless Sensor

This sensor isn't cropped or limited. You're getting the full frame—wide dynamic range, better low-light performance, and razor-sharp images even at high ISO. The lack of a mirror mechanism also means faster shooting, silent modes, and real-time previews of your exposure.

2. Dual Pixel CMOS AF II with Deep Learning

Canon's autofocus system is now powered by artificial intelligence. Instead of just detecting contrast or face patterns, it *learns* to track subjects based on shape, movement, and context. This is game-changing for sports, wildlife, and dynamic human portraits. Your camera becomes intuitive.

3. 8K RAW Video Recording

Yes, it's real—and it's internal. The R5 II records uncompressed 8K RAW or compressed formats, **with** full-frame readout and no crop. This gives you cinematic footage with massive detail, flexibility for reframing, and deep color information for post-processing.

4. IBIS + Lens IS + Digital IS

The holy trinity of stabilization: the sensor moves (IBIS), the lens elements move (Optical IS), and software assists (Digital IS). Together, they create smoothness that was once only possible with gimbals or rigs.

5. Electronic Viewfinder (EVF) Experience

Unlike an optical viewfinder, the EVF shows you exactly what the sensor sees—including exposure, color temperature, focus peaking, zebras, and framing tools. What you see is truly what you get.

Final Thought: Know Your Tool, Unleash Your Vision

The Canon R5 Mark II is not a toy. It's a precision-engineered instrument—a mirrorless beast designed to disappear between you and your vision. But its complexity can be intimidating if you're not guided.

This book was created so that you don't have to guess, Google, or get frustrated. In the next chapters, we'll break down the controls, settings, autofocus mastery, video workflows, and real-world applications so you can shoot anything, anywhere—with full creative confidence.

Now that you've met the beast, let's teach it to roar.

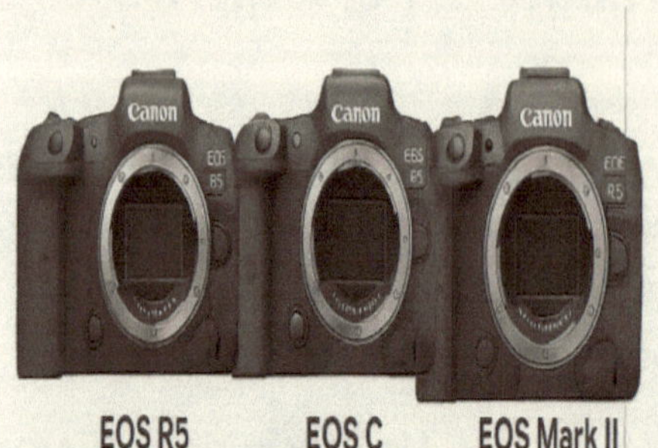

	EOS R5	EOS C	EOS Mark II
	45MP stills	•Lmproved processing	AI Autofocus
	8K/60p RAW	8K60 112 bit RAW	Mitigacted
	Dual DIGIC X	AI autofocus	Refined IBIS mitigated

Spec Simplified

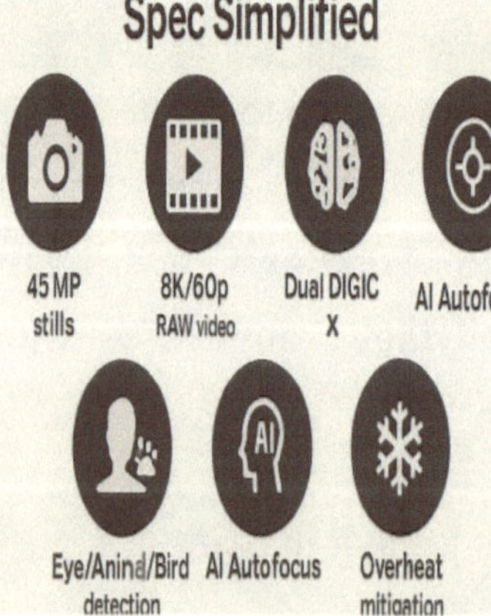

Meet Your R5 Mark II

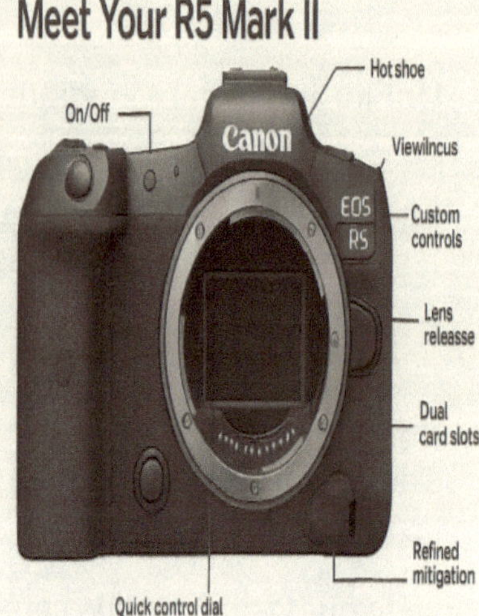

Understanding Mirrorless

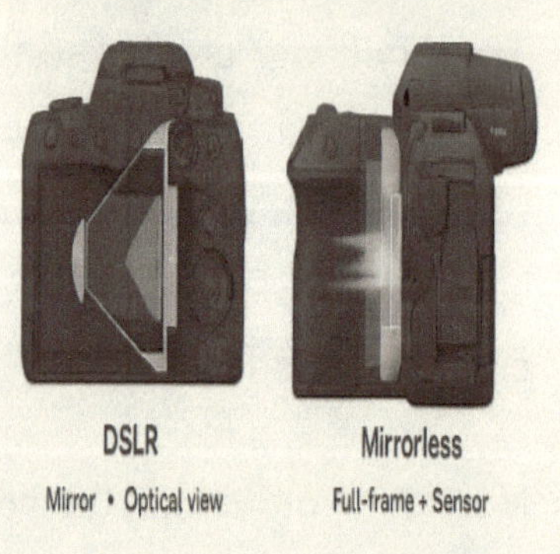

Chapter 2

Unboxing to First Click — Initial Setup

There's something electric about opening the box on a brand-new camera—especially when it's as powerful as the Canon EOS R5 Mark II. You peel back the packaging, lift that sleek body out of its cradle, and feel the weight of possibility in your hands. But then the questions come rushing in. *What now? What do I need to shoot? What settings should I check first?* This chapter is your practical guide to getting the R5 Mark II up and running, from the very first touch to that satisfying first shutter click.

Whether you're a seasoned shooter upgrading your kit or a first-time Canon user, the initial setup process can be simple, clear, and smooth—if you know exactly what to look for.

What You'll Want Before You Start: Recommended Accessories

Before powering on the camera, it's smart to assemble the right gear so you're not held back by missing essentials or performance bottlenecks. Think of these items not as luxuries, but as non-negotiables that elevate your first experience with the camera—and protect your investment.

Memory Cards:

The R5 Mark II features dual card slots: one CFexpress (Type B) and one UHS-II SD card slot. If you're shooting high-resolution stills or any kind of serious video—especially 4K 60p or 8K RAW—you'll absolutely need a **CFexpress card** with high read/write speeds (minimum 400 MB/s write for sustained video). A 256GB or 512GB card is ideal for mixed use. For casual shooting or JPEG-only workflows, a UHS-II SD card will suffice. But trust this—if you plan on using this camera to its full potential, don't cheap out on cards. They're the gateway to your entire creative output.

Batteries:

The R5 Mark II uses the **Canon LP-E6NH battery**, which offers better performance and longer life than the older LP-E6N. One battery is never enough—get at least **two spares**, and make sure your charger is compatible with the newer NH model. For video shooters or all-day sessions, consider a **USB-C PD power bank** or Canon's **DC coupler (dummy battery)** if you're near an outlet.

Lenses:

If you're starting fresh, the **RF 24–105mm f/4 L IS USM** is the gold-standard all-purpose zoom. It's tack sharp, lightweight for an L-series, and covers everything from street shots to interviews. If you're a portrait lover, the RF 85mm f/2 IS Macro or RF 50mm f/1.8 STM will give you stunning background blur and beautiful depth. Wildlife shooters should look toward the RF 100–500mm L, and vloggers will love the RF 16mm f/2.8 for its ultra-wide storytelling.

Protective Essentials:

Don't skip the basics. A high-quality UV or clear filter can save your front lens element from scratches and grime. A screen protector for the articulating LCD, a soft microfiber cloth, and a weather-sealed camera bag round out the essentials. If you plan to record audio, pick up a RØDE or Deity mic, and for stability, a carbon fiber tripod or compact gimbal is a wise addition.

With your gear in place, it's time to bring the camera to life.

Powering On and Initial Configuration

The first time you power on the Canon EOS R5 Mark II, it will prompt you to set up some foundational preferences. This step is often overlooked or rushed, but spending two minutes here will make every photo, video, and menu interaction that much easier down the road.

Start by sliding the On/Off switch located beside the mode dial to the "On" position. You'll be greeted with Canon's clean startup screen and a request to set the date, time, and time zone. Make sure you set the correct year, especially if you plan to organize photos chronologically or sync with multiple cameras later. If you travel often, the time zone feature is critical for accurate file metadata.

Next, select your language preference. English is the default, but Canon supports a broad range of languages globally. Choose one you're most comfortable with—it affects every menu item and system message.

After that, you can dive into your display preferences. Decide whether you want grid overlays on your LCD, histogram displays, or real-time exposure previews in your viewfinder. If you're used to an optical viewfinder from DSLR days, Canon's electronic viewfinder (EVF) might feel different at first. But once you enable exposure simulation, it becomes a massive asset—you'll see exactly how your exposure settings will affect your image *before* you take the shot.

Also consider enabling touch controls, which allow you to tap to focus or swipe through photos like a smartphone. Canon's touchscreen is responsive and intuitive, making it a key part of your shooting experience.

Lastly, don't forget to disable any power-saving timers for your first few sessions. Nothing's more frustrating than the screen going dark while you're trying to learn the layout. You can always re-enable battery-saving features once you're more familiar with the system.

Mounting the Lens, Attaching the Strap, and

Inserting Memory Cards

Now it's time to physically assemble your camera into something shoot-ready.

Mounting a Lens:

Start by removing the body cap from the camera and the rear cap from your lens. You'll see a red dot on the lens and a matching dot on the camera's lens mount. Line up those dots, insert the lens gently into the mount, and rotate it clockwise until you hear a reassuring *click*. That sound means the lens is locked in and ready. Never force a lens—if it resists, stop, realign, and try again.

Attaching the Strap:

The Canon strap that comes in the box is functional, but you might prefer a more comfortable third-party strap for longer sessions. Regardless of brand, thread each end through the metal eyelets on both sides of the camera body, loop it back through the buckle, and double-check for a secure fit. Make sure the strap's length feels balanced when the camera rests on your chest or shoulder. A properly adjusted strap isn't just about comfort—it also protects your gear.

Inserting the Memory Cards:

The memory card door is located on the right side of the camera grip. Slide the latch downward and open the door to reveal two slots. The top slot is for CFexpress cards, and the bottom slot is for UHS-

II SD cards. Insert each card label-forward (facing you). Gently push until you hear a soft click. The card should sit flush with the slot. Close the door firmly until it clicks shut—if it's even slightly ajar, the camera won't power properly.

Now power the camera on again, and you'll see the card format prompt. Always format new cards inside the camera before shooting. This ensures compatibility and optimal file structure for Canon's firmware. Navigate to Menu > Wrench Tab > Format Card, and confirm the operation. Be warned: formatting will erase all data on the card, so never do this with images you haven't backed up.

Your First Click

Now you're ready. The lens is mounted. The battery is charged. The card is formatted. Your date and language are set. And you've got a camera in your hands that can capture the world in jaw-dropping detail.

Take a breath. Look around. Frame a shot through the viewfinder. Use the shutter button to gently focus—and press all the way down. That satisfying click? That's not just a mechanical action. It's the beginning of your creative journey with the Canon EOS R5 Mark II.

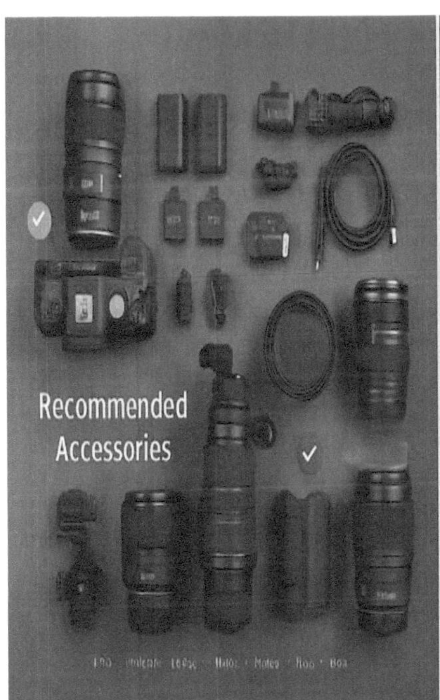

Recommended
Accessories

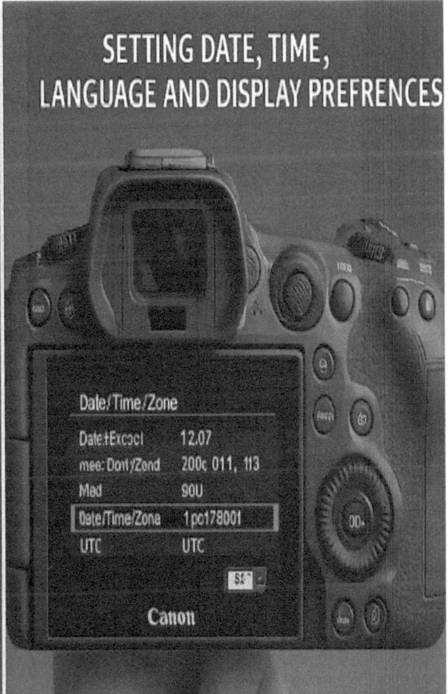

SETTING DATE, TIME,
LANGUAGE AND DISPLAY PREFRENCES
Date/Time/Zone
Canon

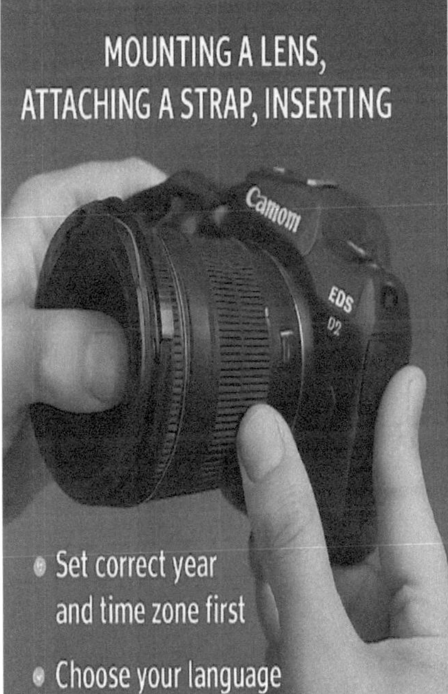

MOUNTING A LENS,
ATTACHING A STRAP, INSERTING
Set correct year
and time zone first
Choose your language

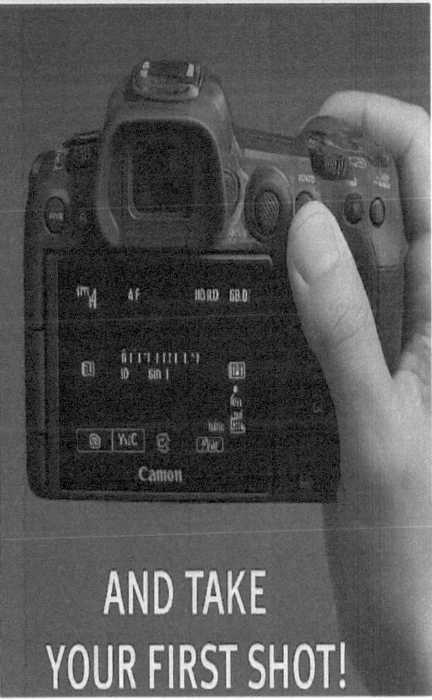

AND TAKE
YOUR FIRST SHOT!

Chapter 3

Demystifying the Menu System

Making the Canon R5 Mark II Work for You—Not Against You

One of the first roadblocks most people hit when using the Canon EOS R5 Mark II is the menu system. It's not that it's poorly designed—Canon's interface is actually one of the more organized in the camera world—but when you combine an insanely powerful sensor, a professional-grade video system, and layers of customization, things can get overwhelming fast.

This chapter is here to put you in the driver's seat. You'll not only understand how the menus are structured, but you'll also learn how to customize them to fit your personal shooting style. By the end of this section, you'll be flying through settings with speed and confidence, adjusting what matters without digging, guessing, or slowing down your creative flow.

Let's start by decoding the structure.

The Logic Behind Canon Menus

Canon organizes its camera settings using a tab-based horizontal menu, visible when you press the Menu button (located near the top-left corner on the back of the camera body). Across the top, you'll see color-coded icons and numbered sections—each representing a category of settings.

The goal of Canon's design is to separate photo settings, video settings, camera functions, and custom options to avoid crowding a single page with unrelated controls. That sounds nice in theory, but without context, it can feel like a sea of acronyms and toggles.

Here's the big idea: Each tab category corresponds to a shooting mode—Photo or Video—and then expands into general camera operation and personalization tools.

Understanding the Main Tabs

Let's break down the core tabs you'll use most often, and what kind of settings live in each.

1. Shooting Settings Tabs (Red Camera Icon)

These tabs appear differently depending on whether you're in Photo Mode or Video Mode. Canon is smart like that—it adjusts the visible settings based on the mode you're currently in.

In Photo Mode, you'll find settings like:

- Image quality (RAW, C-RAW, JPEG)
- Drive mode (single shot, high-speed continuous)
- Silent shutter and anti-flicker
- White balance, picture styles, HDR, and more

In Video Mode, the red camera tabs let you adjust:

- Resolution and frame rate (8K, 4K HQ, Full HD)
- Compression type (RAW, IPB, ALL-I)
- Canon Log profiles (LOG, LOG 3)
- Audio input levels and headphone monitoring
- Movie servo AF, focus peaking, zebra patterns

2. Autofocus Tab (Purple AF Icon)

This is where the real magic happens for focus customization.

Here you'll control:

- Subject detection type (human, animal, vehicle)

- Eye detection behavior
- Servo AF responsiveness and tracking sensitivity
- Touch-and-drag AF setup
- Focus peaking and MF assist (especially useful for video)

If you ever find that the autofocus is "not acting the way I want it to," this is the first place to check.

3. Playback Tab (Blue Playback Icon)

This section handles how images and videos are reviewed after capture. It's more about personal preference, but settings here include:

- Image display time
- Auto rotate and slideshow options
- Magnification settings (great for checking focus)
- Protect/delete functions for batch review

4. Set-up Tab (Yellow Wrench Icon)

Arguably one of the most critical areas of the menu. This is where you manage:

- Card formatting
- Date/time settings
- Display brightness and EVF behavior
- Power saving and auto shut-off timers

- Firmware updates
- USB mode (important for live streaming or tethering)
- HDMI output settings

Don't underestimate this section—it's foundational to keeping your camera reliable and optimized.

5. Custom Functions Tab (Orange Camera with Gear Icon)

Here you'll find the deep personalization features that let you tailor the R5 Mark II to your hand and brain. You can:

- Remap buttons
- Adjust control wheel behavior
- Program C1, C2, and C3 custom shooting modes
- Configure dial directions for exposure compensation
- Set safety shift and shutter-release priority

6. My Menu Tab (Green Star Icon)

This is your shortcut headquarters. We'll dive deeper into this in a moment, but just know this: My Menu is where your workflow transforms from default to professional.

How to Customize "My Menu" for Fast Access

The "My Menu" tab is Canon's most underutilized power feature—and it's a game-changer for speeding up your workflow. Instead of digging through ten tabs every time you want to adjust autofocus tracking or switch from 4K HQ to 4K 60p, you can put those options right at your fingertips.

Here's how to build your My Menu like a pro:

1. Navigate to the green star tab.
2. Choose "Register settings to My Menu" or "Add My Menu Tab."
3. Select frequently used settings from any part of the main menu. Think:
   - Format card
   - Image quality
   - White balance
   - Movie recording size
   - Subject detection
   - Eye AF toggle
   - Customize buttons
   - Canon Log profile toggle
4. You can create multiple tabs if one isn't enough. For instance:
   - **Tab 1**: Your core stills settings
   - **Tab 2**: Your core video settings

- ○ **Tab 3**: Workflow tools (format card, connect to smartphone)

5. Once you've added your items, you can reorder them or delete ones you no longer use.

Think of this as building your own personal dashboard. Every time you press the Menu button, you can have exactly what you need—no scrolling, no second-guessing.

Real-World Walkthrough: Building a Custom Menu for Photo & Video

Let's say you're a hybrid shooter—someone who photographs clients during the day and captures content for social or YouTube at night. Here's how you might set up your My Menu tabs for speed and sanity:

For Photography:

- Image Quality: RAW + JPEG
- Drive Mode: High-Speed Continuous+
- Subject Detection: Eye (Human)
- White Balance: Auto + Kelvin Adjust
- Format Card
- Customize Buttons

For Video:

- Movie Recording Size: 4K HQ / 60p
- Canon Log: Enable / Disable
- Audio Levels: Manual
- Zebra Pattern: On (95%)
- Movie Servo AF: Enable
- Subject Detection: Eye + Animal

For Workflow:

- Format Card (again, because you always forget)
- Connect to Smartphone
- Clean HDMI Output Settings
- Screen Brightness

This setup allows you to move from portrait session to product B-roll shoot in under 15 seconds, without having to reset your entire camera.

Final Thoughts: Make the Camera Serve You

The Canon R5 Mark II is a masterpiece of engineering, but it's also a tool—and any tool is only as powerful as your ability to use it intuitively. Once you internalize the menu layout and build your custom menu system, the camera starts to disappear between you and the art you're trying to create.

Don't be intimidated by the options. Embrace them. Learn your camera the way a musician learns their instrument—until every dial, every setting, and every screen becomes an extension of your intent.

DEMYSTIFYING THE MENU SYSTEM

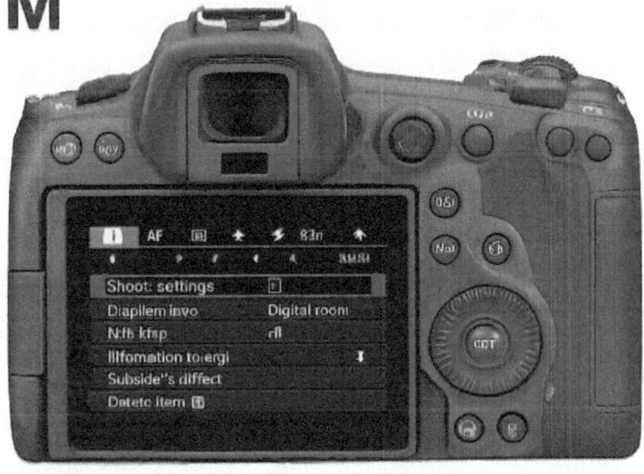

UNDERSTANDING TABS

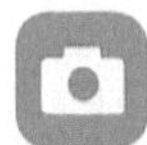 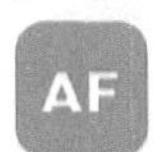   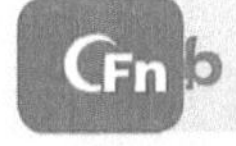 

PHOTO VIDEO AF PLAYBACK SET-UP MY MENU

CUSTOMIZING 'MY MENU'

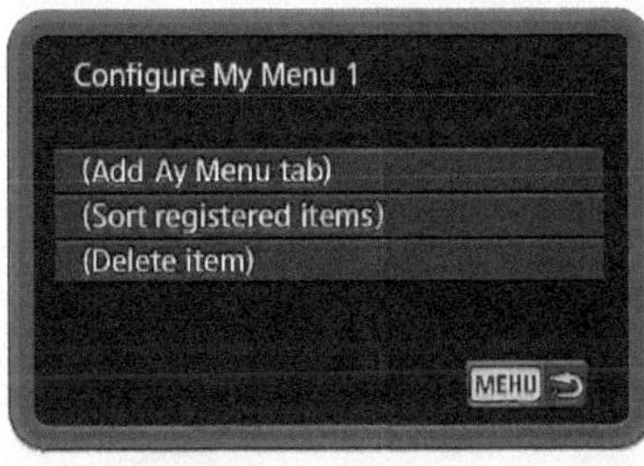

- Store your most-used settings for quick access
- Registrable items: Image quality, exposure settings, movie rec quality and more

EXAMPLE: SETTINGS FOR PHOTOGRAPHY & VIDEO

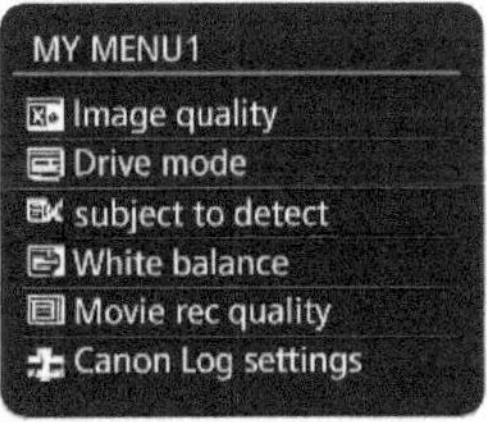

Image quality

Drive mode

Subject to detect

White balance

Part II: Mastering Photography With The R5 Mark II

Chapter 4

Understanding Autofocus Like a Pro

Turning Precision Into Second Nature

The Canon EOS R5 Mark II doesn't just focus—it thinks. With a next-gen Dual Pixel CMOS AF II system powered by deep learning and AI-based subject recognition, this camera can identify, track, and lock onto your subject with uncanny precision. Whether you're capturing a bride walking down the aisle, a child spinning in circles at sunset, or a hawk in flight against a bright sky, the R5 Mark II isn't just reacting—it's anticipating.

But that power comes with complexity. If you've ever found yourself frustrated with the autofocus system hunting, missing, or locking onto the wrong part of the scene, this chapter will be your breakthrough moment.

Autofocus is where your camera either becomes an extension of your eye—or fights you. Let's make sure it's the former.

Subject Detection Explained: Teaching the

Camera What to Look For

At the heart of the R5 Mark II's autofocus system is its subject detection engine—and it's a beast.

Using a sophisticated AI model, the camera can identify and prioritize different kinds of subjects in real-time. You can manually select what kind of subject you're working with, allowing the autofocus system to zero in faster and more reliably. Here's what each detection mode does:

- **Human**: Tracks faces, eyes, heads, and torsos. Even if the subject turns away or is wearing a mask, the camera maintains focus.
- **Eye**: Zooms in on the most critical detail—your subject's eye. If the eye disappears, it falls back to face, then head, then body.
- **Animal**: Ideal for dogs, cats, horses, and most four-legged companions. It detects body outlines and faces even in motion.
- **Bird**: Specialized tracking for birds in flight, including small species with rapid wing movement or against cluttered skies.
- **Vehicle**: Tracks cars, motorcycles, and racing vehicles. It can detect front, rear, or entire vehicles depending on movement and framing.

If you leave subject detection on "Auto," the camera will attempt to guess the subject—but in practice, manual subject selection yields better results. If you're shooting a person, choose Human. If you're photographing wildlife, switch to Animal or Bird. This small step can prevent frustration later.

Autofocus Modes and When to Use Them

Autofocus is more than subject detection—it's also about how the system behaves in different shooting environments. The R5 Mark II offers several AF modes, each suited for a specific kind of motion or shooting style.

Here's how they break down:

One-Shot AF

Best for still subjects—portraits, landscapes, product shots. Once focus is acquired, it locks and doesn't adjust further unless you refocus. Great when your subject isn't moving.

Servo AF (Continuous)

Essential for moving subjects. The camera continuously adjusts focus as the subject moves toward or away from the lens. Ideal for sports, wildlife, events, or video work. Combined with subject detection, Servo AF becomes an intelligent tracking system.

Manual AF Area Selection Options

Within these main modes, you can choose how broad or precise the autofocus area should be:

- **Face + Tracking AF**: Most intelligent and automatic. Great for people, events, or dynamic framing.
- **Spot AF**: For pinpoint accuracy—useful in macro photography or low-light shooting.
- **1-Point AF**: Standard single point. Good for focusing on off-center subjects or shooting through obstacles.
- **Expand AF Area**: Adds helper points around your chosen AF point to assist with tracking.
- **Zone AF**: Larger rectangular group of points—ideal for unpredictable subjects or when you need to cover a general area.
- **Whole Area AF**: Uses the full autofocus grid—perfect for subject tracking in Servo AF.

How to Set Up Eye-Detect AF for Portraits

Few things are more satisfying than capturing tack-sharp eyes in a portrait. The R5 Mark II's Eye AF makes this easier than ever—if you set it up properly.

Here's a simple step-by-step to enable flawless Eye Detection for portraits:

1. Switch to Photo Mode (or Video if doing a talking-head or interview style shoot).
2. Press Menu, go to the AF tab (purple icon).
3. Under Subject to Detect, select Human.
4. Enable Eye Detection AF.
5. Under AF Method, choose Face + Tracking AF.
6. If you're shooting wide open (e.g. f/1.2–f/2), make sure your shutter speed is high enough (1/250s or faster) to avoid motion blur that looks like missed focus.

Once you've done this, simply half-press the shutter or use your back-button focus (more on that in a moment), and the camera will find and cling to your subject's eye like magic—even if they move, turn, or step in and out of light.

Button Mapping for Back Button Focus (BBF)

Back Button Focus is one of the most powerful techniques you can adopt to gain more control over your focus system. Instead of using the shutter button to both focus and shoot, BBF separates these two actions. It's incredibly useful when:

- Your subject moves unpredictably
- You want to focus once and recompose
- You're shooting with Servo AF and want better control over when tracking starts

Here's how to set it up on the R5 Mark II:

1. Press Menu > Custom Functions (orange camera + gear icon).
2. Navigate to Customize Buttons.
3. Locate the AF-ON button and set it to Metering + AF Start.
4. Set the Shutter Button Half-Press to Metering Start Only (this disables autofocus from the shutter).
5. Optionally, assign Eye Detection Toggle or AF Area Selection to another nearby button for quick adjustments on the fly.

Now, focusing becomes a deliberate act. You press the back button to acquire focus—then shoot as many frames as you like, without the camera constantly refocusing. It's the secret sauce of wedding photographers, sports shooters, and wildlife pros alike.

Troubleshooting: When Autofocus Hunts, Misses, or Struggles

Even with cutting-edge tech, autofocus can stumble. Here are the most common autofocus issues R5 Mark II users face—and how to fix them fast.

Problem: Focus Hunts in Low Light

Fix:

- Use a lens with a wider aperture (f/2.8 or lower) to let in more light.
- Increase ISO to make the scene brighter.
- Use a focus assist beam (from an external flash) or switch to 1-Point AF to give the system something to lock onto.

Problem: Focus Locks on the Background

Fix:

- Narrow your AF area. Switch from "Whole Area" to "Spot" or "1-Point AF."
- Enable Face + Eye Detection to override the system's bias toward contrasty backgrounds.

Problem: Camera Tracks the Wrong Subject

Fix:

- Don't use "Auto" subject detection unless absolutely necessary.
- Manually choose Human, Animal, or Vehicle based on your scene.

- Use the Touchscreen to manually select your subject when Face + Tracking is active.

Problem: Eye AF Doesn't Engage

Fix:

- Make sure Face + Tracking is selected, not 1-Point or Zone AF.
- Confirm that Eye Detection AF is turned ON in the AF menu.
- Eyes must be visible, well-lit, and relatively close—at extreme distances or poor lighting, the camera may fall back to face or head.

Problem: Tracking Drops Mid-Shot

Fix:

- Enable AF Case 2 in the Servo AF settings (good for erratic subjects).
- Increase Tracking Sensitivity to prioritize the subject you're already following.

Final Word: Autofocus Is a Dance—Learn Its Rhythm

The Canon R5 Mark II's autofocus system is nothing short of phenomenal—but like any powerful tool, it demands understanding.

Learn how to communicate clearly with it. Set it up with intention. Use the right modes for the right moments. And when something doesn't work, know which lever to pull to bring it back in line.

Autofocus isn't just about getting the image sharp—it's about capturing the decisive moment with zero hesitation. Once you master this system, your focus becomes instinct, not guesswork. Your camera sees what you see.

UNDERSTANDING AUTOFOCUS LIKE A PRO

Subject Detection Explained

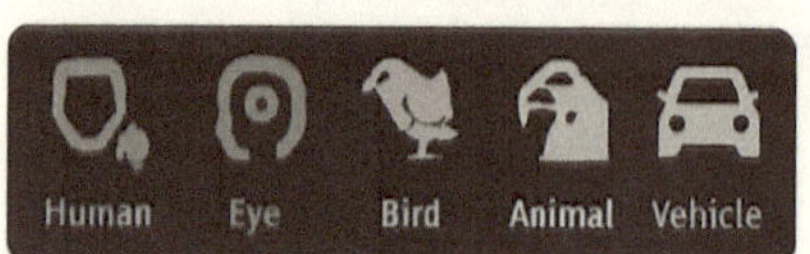

The RS Mark II can detect various subjects on **humans, animals, birds, and vehicles** — as well as

AF Modes and When to Use Them

One Shot AF

Subject to detect
Locks focus on still subjects

Servo AF
Manuaauand rama AF

Servo AF

Set AF method
to Face + Tracking AF

Manual
AF area select options

Manual AF area selection options

- Assig: Human for Face + Tracking AF
- Enable Eye detection AF

Button Mapping for Back Button Focus

Back button focus: separates AF-ON from shutter button for added control

- Assign AF-ON button as ◀◀AF-start
- Change *Shutter button nulf-press to Metering start*

How to Set Up Eye-Detect AF for Portraits

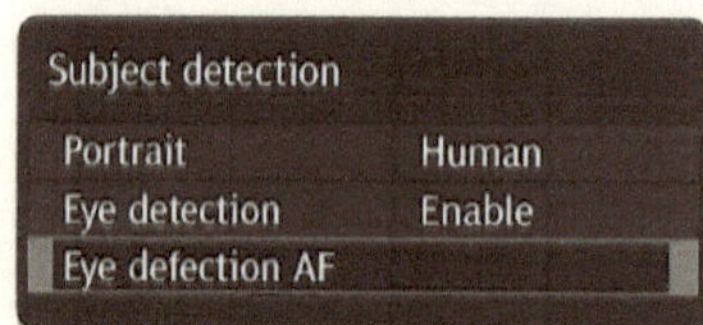

1 Select **Human** for Subject to detect
2 Set AF method to **Face + Tracking AF**
3 Enable Eye detection AF

Troubleshooting: When AF Hunts or Misses

Troubleshooting: When AF Hunts or Misses

- Select the appropriate detection mode
- Activate tracking with the shutter or AF-ON button

Chapter 5

Taming the Exposure Triangle with Canon Controls

The Power to Paint With Light, in the Palm of Your Hands

Mastering exposure is the heartbeat of photography. It's where science meets intuition. And while modern cameras like the Canon EOS R5 Mark II are packed with intelligent auto modes, the magic really begins when *you* take control.

This chapter will walk you through the exposure triangle—shutter speed, aperture, and ISO—in simple, plain English. You'll learn how these three elements interact, how to master them using Canon's intuitive controls, and how to read your camera's feedback (like the histogram and highlight warnings) to make confident, deliberate decisions about light and mood.

Whether you're shooting dreamy portraits at golden hour, crisp action shots, or moody video in low light, the knowledge you gain here will free you from guesswork and give you command over the image you envision.

Shutter Speed, Aperture, ISO: Simple Language

Let's begin with the exposure triangle. Think of it as a three-way balancing act that determines how bright or dark your image appears—and just as importantly, how it feels.

Shutter Speed

This controls how long the camera's sensor is exposed to light. It's measured in fractions of a second (like 1/1000s) or full seconds (like 1", 2", etc.).

- **Faster shutter speeds (1/1000s, 1/2000s)** freeze motion—ideal for sports, wildlife, or handheld shots in bright light.
- **Slower shutter speeds (1/30s, 1/4s, 1")** allow more light in but blur motion—great for waterfalls, light trails, or night photography with a tripod.

Think of shutter speed as controlling motion. It answers the question: *Should this moment feel frozen or flowing?*

Aperture (f-stop)

This refers to the size of the opening in the lens. It controls how much light passes through and how much of the image is in focus.

- **Wider apertures (f/1.2, f/2.8)** = more light + shallower depth of field = soft backgrounds, dreamy bokeh, focus on one subject.
- **Narrower apertures (f/8, f/11, f/16)** = less light + deeper focus = landscapes, architecture, group shots.

Aperture controls depth and emotion. It answers: *What should be sharp, and what should melt away?*

ISO

This adjusts the sensor's sensitivity to light.

- **Lower ISO (100–400)** = cleanest image quality, minimal noise. Best in bright environments.
- **Higher ISO (1600–12800+)** = brighter images in low light, but with increased grain/noise.

ISO is your light booster. When your shutter and aperture can't do it all, ISO steps in. But use it with care—the higher you go, the more digital texture you introduce.

Manual Mode Walkthrough

Manual mode gives you full control over all three elements. It might seem intimidating at first, but the Canon R5 Mark II makes it surprisingly intuitive. Here's a step-by-step guide to getting comfortable.

1. **Set the Mode Dial to "M" (Manual).**

   This frees all three variables—shutter speed, aperture, and ISO—for manual adjustment.

2. **Control Each Setting with Dials:**
   - Use the top main dial to adjust shutter speed.
   - Use the rear dial near the thumb to control aperture.
   - Use the multi-function button (M-Fn) and scroll to ISO, or assign ISO to a custom button for quick access.

3. **Use the Light Meter on Your Display or Viewfinder.**

   As you adjust each setting, you'll see a scale from –3 to +3. Aim to keep your exposure around 0 (center) unless you're going for a specific creative look (e.g., underexposed silhouette or bright high-key).

4. **Take a Test Shot.**

   Review your image and adjust accordingly. If the image is too dark, either:
   - Slow the shutter
   - Open the aperture (lower f-number)
   - Raise the ISO

If it's too bright, do the opposite.

5. **Use Live View for Real-Time Feedback.**

   The R5 Mark II's EVF and LCD show live exposure

simulation. What you see is what you get—so adjust visually, not just numerically.

Auto ISO Limits & Exposure Compensation

Manual control doesn't always mean doing everything manually. Smart use of Auto ISO lets you focus on shutter and aperture while the camera maintains consistent exposure.

Setting Up Auto ISO Properly

1. Go to the Shooting Menu and locate ISO settings.
2. Set ISO to Auto.
3. Define your Minimum and Maximum ISO range:
     - For daylight: Min 100, Max 1600
     - For low light: Min 100, Max 6400 or 12800

Now, the camera will raise ISO only when needed, within your chosen bounds.

This is perfect for situations like:

- Events with rapidly changing light
- Handheld video where shutter and aperture need to remain fixed
- Street photography, where speed matters more than control

If you're using Auto ISO, Aperture Priority (Av)**, or** Shutter Priority (Tv) modes, the camera controls part of the triangle for you—but you still need to communicate your creative intent.

That's where Exposure Compensation comes in. It lets you tell the camera:

"Yes, I know this exposure is 'technically correct'—but I want it brighter/darker."

Rotate the rear dial while looking through the EVF or use the Q menu to adjust exposure compensation:

- **+1 EV** = brighter
- **−1 EV** = darker

This is great for:

- Silhouettes at sunset (dial negative)
- High-key portraits or white backgrounds (dial positive)
- Correcting a camera that always exposes skin too dark or bright

How to Read Your Histogram and Highlight

Alerts

Relying on just the screen can fool you—especially in bright sunlight or dim environments. That's why learning to read the histogram is one of the most empowering habits you can develop as a photographer or videographer.

What is a Histogram?

A histogram is a graphical representation of brightness in your image, from shadows (left) to highlights (right).

- A peak on the left = dark shadows
- A peak in the middle = midtones
- A peak on the right = bright highlights

Your goal is usually to avoid:

- **Clipping blacks** (piling up on the far left) → crushed shadows, no detail
- **Clipping whites** (piling up on the far right) → blown highlights, unrecoverable

How to Use It in the Field

Enable the histogram overlay (in live view or playback). As you adjust your settings:

- If the graph is too far left, you're underexposed.
- If it's too far right, you're overexposed.
- A good histogram is often *balanced*, with data spread across.

There's no perfect shape—it depends on your subject. A night shot might lean left. A beach scene might lean right.

Highlight Alert (Blinkies)

Enable Highlight Alert in the playback menu. Now, when you review an image, any blown-out areas will blink white. This is your warning: detail is gone in those areas. Reduce exposure next time to preserve information.

This is especially helpful for:

- Wedding dresses
- Sunlit clouds
- Bright backgrounds behind your subject

Final Word: Control Light, Control Emotion

Understanding exposure isn't about memorizing numbers—it's about learning to paint with light. Once you know how shutter speed shapes time, how aperture sculpts focus, and how ISO dances with shadows, you stop reacting and start creating.

With the Canon R5 Mark II, these tools are not just accessible—they're tactile, responsive, and elegantly designed to let you stay in flow. You can feel your way through a shoot without taking your eye off the viewfinder. And that is the mark of a true creative instrument.

Shutter Speed, Aperture, ISO

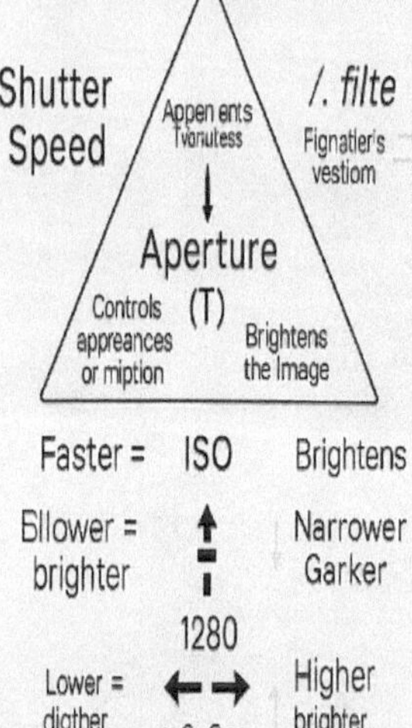

Manual Mode Walkthrough

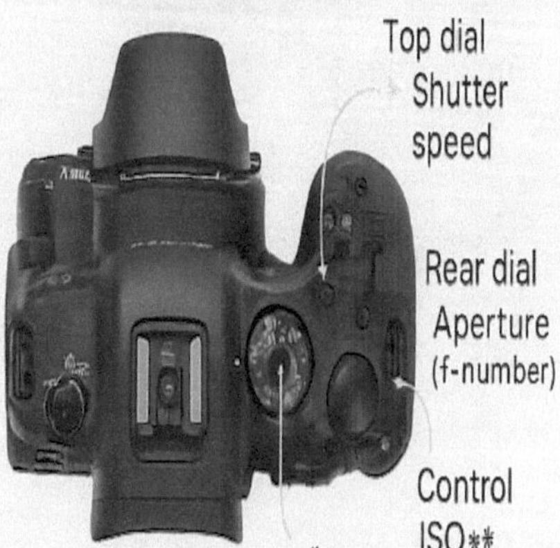

Adjust each setting to get the desired exposure

Auto ISO Limits & Exposure Compensation

Go to:

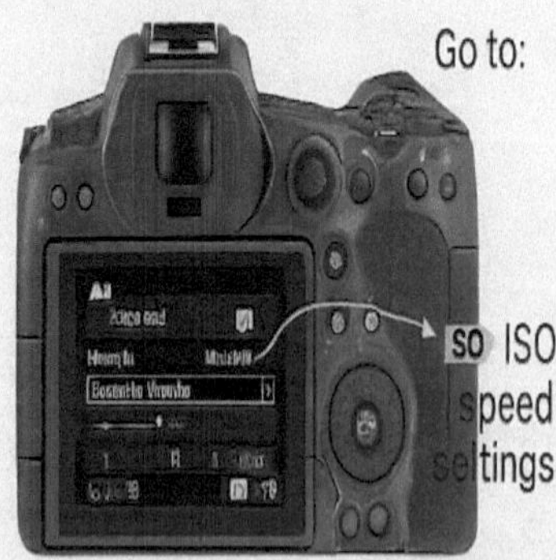

Set Auto range (e.g. 100-6400)

How to Read Your Histogram

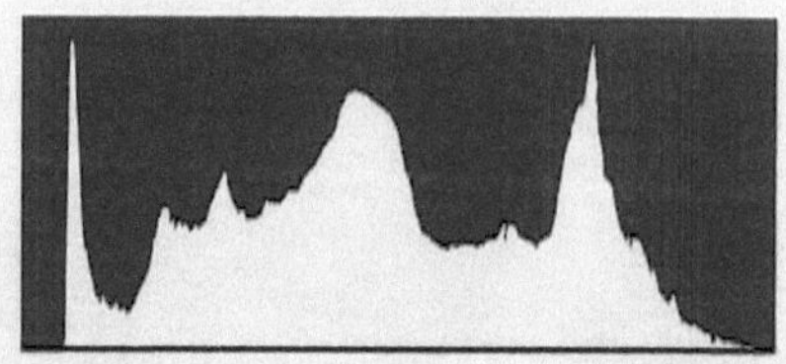

Shadows   Midtones   Highlights

Dark < Exposure > Bright

⚠ Enable Highlight alert
Looks for clipped areas

Chapter 6

Picture Styles, White Balance & In-Camera Looks

Crafting Your Signature Aesthetic Without Post-Processing

Not every photographer wants to spend hours in Lightroom or DaVinci Resolve. And with the power packed into the Canon EOS R5 Mark II, you don't have to. This camera gives you remarkable control over the final image *before* you ever touch a computer screen. With the right use of Picture Styles, White Balance, **and** in-camera customization tools, you can craft rich, cinematic, or true-to-life photos and videos that are ready to share the moment they're captured.

Whether you're a SOOC JPEG shooter, a hybrid content creator, or a professional looking to create a consistent look across sessions, this chapter will show you how to get the most out of your images straight out of camera.

Let's unlock the color, tone, and feeling that make your work yours.

Choosing a Look: Picture Styles Explained

Picture Styles are Canon's version of color profiles—predefined sets of contrast, sharpness, saturation, and tone curves that affect the final look of your JPEGs or the preview of your RAW files.

They don't affect the sensor data in RAW mode, but they do change:

- What you see on the LCD/EVF
- How JPEGs and video footage appear
- How your RAW previews are displayed in-camera and in some editing software

Here's a breakdown of the built-in styles and when to use them:

Portrait

Designed to deliver soft skin tones, gentle contrast, and flattering color. Ideal for headshots, couples, weddings, and baby photography. Avoids oversharpening, which can be unkind to facial features.

Landscape

Boosts blues and greens, adds contrast, and sharpens details. Perfect for scenes with rich skies, trees, or architectural shots. This is your go-to for vivid travel or outdoor work.

Faithful

Replicates colors under standard daylight (5200K) as accurately as possible. Great for product photography, artwork reproduction, or studio setups where accurate color representation is critical.

Neutral

Flatter and less saturated than Standard. Keeps details in highlights and shadows. Excellent base for post-processing and subtle documentary-style shooting.

Standard

This is Canon's default—good for everyday shooting, but often too contrasty or saturated for professional use. Consider switching to Neutral or Portrait if you're seeking a more natural look.

Monochrome

Black and white conversion in-camera. Offers filters like Red, Yellow, Green to manipulate tones. Great for testing compositions, focusing on shape/light, or shooting timeless street photos.

User-Defined (Custom 1, 2, 3)

You can create your own style by adjusting:

- **Sharpness**: Use less for portraits, more for landscapes
- **Contrast**: Lower for gentle scenes, higher for drama
- **Saturation**: Personal taste—avoid cranking it unless going for stylized looks
- **Color tone**: Adjust to warm or cool slightly for your vibe

Pro Tip: If you're shooting JPEGs for delivery or previews (e.g. weddings, events, client proofs), building your own custom Picture Style can drastically cut down your editing time—or eliminate it altogether.

White Balance: Natural Light vs Studio Light

White balance (WB) controls how your camera interprets color temperature—whether the image skews warm (orange/yellow) or cool (blue). Getting WB right in-camera makes skin tones natural, products accurate, and skies believable.

Auto White Balance (AWB)

Great for general shooting, and it has improved in the R5 Mark II. But under mixed lighting, AWB can swing inconsistently from shot to shot. You might end up with warm skin in one photo and cool skin in the next, especially indoors.

Canon now gives you two AWB modes:

- **AWB Priority (White)**: Removes warm tones for accurate whites—good for studio/product work
- **AWB Priority (Ambience)**: Retains a bit of warmth for mood—better for natural light, cozy scenes

Preset White Balance Modes

Use these to match common lighting environments:

- **Daylight (5200K)** – Use in sun or white LED lights
- **Shade (7000K)** – Warms up cool shadows
- **Cloudy (6000K)** – Adds warmth on overcast days
- **Tungsten (3200K)** – Cools down warm indoor bulbs
- **Fluorescent (4000K)** – Neutralizes green/blue tint from fluorescent lights
- **Flash (6000K)** – Optimized for Canon speedlites

Kelvin Temperature (K Mode)

If you want precise control, dial in a Kelvin value manually. This is invaluable in studio settings where lighting is constant and controlled.

- Set to 5200K for neutral daylight
- Increase to 6000–7000K for warm light (sunset, shade)
- Decrease to 3200–4000K for cool light (tungsten, night)

Custom White Balance

Use a white or gray card to manually calibrate WB. Essential for commercial, catalog, or color-critical work. Take a test shot of the reference card, then select it under the Custom WB menu.

Best Settings for SOOC (Straight Out of Camera) JPEG Shooters

If you prefer to shoot JPEG and want your images to look polished straight from the camera—no editing software required—here are key steps to dial in your R5 Mark II for SOOC excellence.

1. Set Picture Style with Intention

Portrait shooters: Choose "Portrait" and reduce sharpness slightly
Landscape lovers: Choose "Landscape" and boost saturation modestly
General shooters: Start with "Neutral" and create your own balanced style under User 1

2. Use Fine-Tuned White Balance

Avoid leaving WB on Auto in mixed-light settings. Instead:

- Use presets for consistent results

- Use Kelvin or custom WB if consistency across images matters

3. Adjust JPEG Parameters in Picture Style

Go to Picture Style > Detail Set > and modify:

- Sharpness (lower for skin, higher for texture-rich scenes)
- Contrast (reduce slightly for smoother tones)
- Saturation (adjust to taste)
- Color tone (subtle warm or cool shift)

Save this as a User Defined Picture Style for fast access. You'll notice your JPEGs already feel edited.

4. Enable Lens Corrections in Camera

Turn on in-camera corrections for:

- Vignetting
- Chromatic aberration
- Distortion

These will be baked into your JPEGs, giving you polished edges, true lines, and cleaner detail.

5. Highlight Tone Priority (HTP)

Enabling this setting preserves detail in bright areas like white dresses, clouds, or sunlit skin. It slightly reduces highlight exposure and enhances dynamic range—great for weddings, events, or beach scenes.

6. Watch the Histogram While Shooting

Keep highlights from blowing out and ensure balanced exposure by enabling the histogram overlay in live view. Combined with your picture style, it gives you a live preview of how your JPEG will render.

7. Use Creative Filters for Stylized JPEGs *(Optional)*

For fun or unique looks, experiment with:

- Grainy B/W
- Soft Focus
- Toy Camera effect
  These are applied to JPEGs only and can be great for stylized sets, Instagram-friendly images, or creative client delivery.

Final Word: Make the Camera Do the Work

The Canon EOS R5 Mark II gives you the tools of a professional editing suite, built right into the camera. Whether you're delivering JPEGs to a client, sharing behind-the-scenes images instantly, or just prefer to shoot and share, this chapter empowers you to build your own aesthetic with intention and precision—no Photoshop required.

When you treat color, tone, and exposure as tools of storytelling, every image you create becomes more than just a capture—it becomes a signature. And that, more than any lens or spec, is what sets great creators apart.

CHAPTER 6: PICTURE STYLES, WHITE BALANCE & IN-CAMERA LOOKS

Crafting Your Signature Aesthetic Without Post-Processing

Choosing a Look: Picture Styles Explained

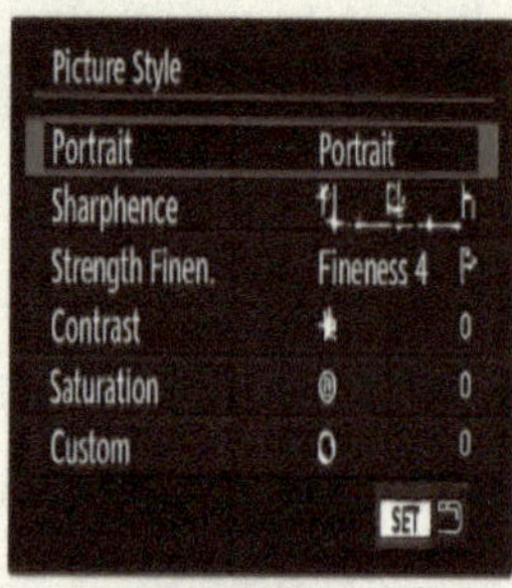

- **Portrait**   ideal for people, smoothes skin tones

- **Landscape**   enhances colors, sharpens edges

- **Faithful**   accurate colors under daylight

- **Neutral**   natural look, lower contrast

- **Custom**   create your own style

White Balance: Natural Light vs Studio Light

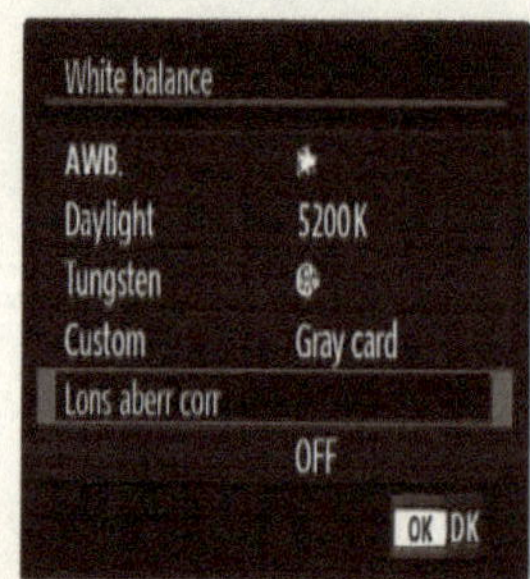

- **AWB**   automatic, useful for mixed lighting

- **Daylight**   sunny outdoors

- **Tungsten**   corrects orange cast from indoor lights

- **Custom**   gray card works in any light

Best Settings for JPEG Shooters

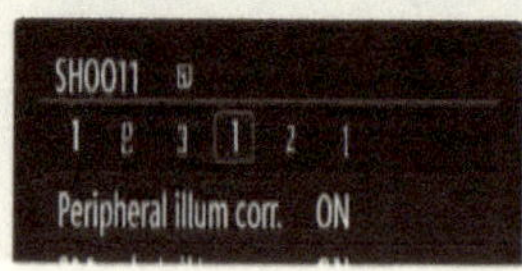

- Pick a picture style that fits your **subject**

- Fine-tune **WB** instead of relying on AWB

Chapter 7

Real-Life Photo Recipes

Shoot With Confidence in Any Situation

By now, you've learned how to control the Canon EOS R5 Mark II, from autofocus wizardry to exposure mastery and picture style tuning. But learning theory is one thing—knowing what to do *in the moment* is something else entirely.

This chapter gives you ready-to-use, real-world shooting setups for popular scenarios: weddings, wildlife, street photography, studio portraits, and low-light scenes. Each "recipe" includes not just technical settings, but also guidance on mindset, gear pairing, and how to work with the light you have. Whether you're a pro on assignment or a passionate hobbyist chasing a great shot, these setups will help you act quickly and shoot deliberately.

Let's step into the real world—and shoot like it.

Wedding Settings For Sharp, Romantic Images

Weddings are fast-paced, high-stakes, and filled with diverse lighting conditions. Your gear must be versatile. Your focus must be precise. And your images? They should feel timeless, tender, and true.

Recommended Mode: Manual or Aperture Priority (Av)
Shutter Speed: 1/200s (faster for motion or dancing)
Aperture: f/1.8 to f/2.8 for dreamy backgrounds
ISO: Auto, with a max limit of 6400
White Balance: AWB (Ambience Priority) or set to 5200K in consistent light
Picture Style: Portrait or User-Defined with lowered contrast and sharpness
Autofocus: Face + Eye Detection (Human), Servo AF enabled
Drive Mode: High-Speed Continuous+
Lens Pairings: RF 50mm f/1.2L, RF 85mm f/1.2L, RF 28–70mm f/2L

Key Tip: Use back-button focus for greater control during the ceremony and first look. For group shots, switch to One-Shot AF and increase aperture to f/4 or higher for sufficient depth of field.

Bonus Tip: Enable Highlight Tone Priority to preserve detail in white dresses under sun or flash.

Wildlife Setup With Eye-Tracking For Birds

Photographing birds is a technical and physical challenge. The R5 Mark II's advanced subject tracking and fast burst capabilities make it a powerful tool for this demanding genre—if set up properly.

Recommended Mode: Manual or Shutter Priority (Tv)

Shutter Speed: 1/1600s or faster to freeze wings

Aperture: f/5.6 to f/8 for more depth and sharp detail

ISO: Auto, Max 6400 (or 12800 in dim light)

White Balance: Daylight or Cloudy

Picture Style: Standard or Landscape for vibrancy

Autofocus: Subject to Detect = Bird, AF Area = Whole Area + Servo AF

Drive Mode: High-Speed Continuous+

Lens Pairings: RF 100–500mm f/4.5–7.1L IS USM, EF 600mm f/4 with RF adapter

Key Tip: Set a custom button (like the M-Fn) to instantly toggle between "Bird" and "Human" detection in case another subject enters the frame.

Bonus Tip: Use a monopod or tripod collar to reduce fatigue during long shoots.

Street Photography Setup For Fast Reaction

Street photography is about anticipation, subtlety, and readiness. You can't ask your subjects to pause. You must shoot discreetly, intuitively, and fast. This is where the R5 Mark II's silent shutter and compact lenses shine.

Recommended Mode: Aperture Priority (Av) or Manual
Shutter Speed: 1/500s for movement, slower for static subjects
Aperture: f/2.8 to f/5.6 depending on lens and light
ISO: Auto, Max 6400
White Balance: AWB or set to 5200K
Picture Style: Monochrome (for B&W), Neutral or User Defined
Autofocus: Face + Tracking, Eye Detection ON, Servo AF
Drive Mode: Silent Continuous (Low)
Lens Pairings: RF 35mm f/1.8, RF 24–105mm f/4, RF 50mm f/1.8

Key Tip: Turn on silent electronic shutter for complete discretion. No clicks, no attention.

Bonus Tip: Use your camera's touch-and-drag AF or pre-focus at a zone and wait for the subject to enter.

Studio Portraits With Manual Flash

Studio shooting gives you control over light, but demands precision and planning. When using strobes or speedlites, you'll be working in Manual Mode, and your exposure triangle behaves differently.

Recommended Mode: Manual

Shutter Speed: 1/160s (flash sync speed)

Aperture: f/8 to f/11 for sharp detail across face

ISO: 100–200 for clean base image

White Balance: Flash or Custom with gray card

Picture Style: Faithful or Portrait, with low contrast and sharpening

Autofocus: One-Shot AF, Eye Detection ON

Drive Mode: Single shot

Lens Pairings: RF 85mm f/1.2L, RF 70–200mm f/2.8L, RF 50mm f/1.2L

Key Tip: Use modeling lamps to help AF lock in dim studio settings. Consider switching to MF once locked to prevent refocusing.

Bonus Tip: For tethered shooting, connect via USB-C to Canon EOS Utility or Capture One for instant feedback and control.

Low Light Photography Settings And Noise

Reduction Tips

Shooting in low light doesn't mean sacrificing quality. The R5 Mark II has excellent high-ISO performance, and with the right balance, you can walk away with clean, atmospheric images without flash.

Recommended Mode: Manual or Aperture Priority
Shutter Speed: 1/60s to 1/200s handheld; slower on tripod
Aperture: f/1.2 to f/2.8 (wide apertures help here)
ISO: 3200–12800 depending on light level
White Balance: AWB or Kelvin 3200–4000 for indoor tungsten
Picture Style: Neutral or Custom with lower contrast
Autofocus: Face + Tracking, Servo AF with Eye Detection
Drive Mode: Silent or Silent Continuous
Lens Pairings: RF 50mm f/1.2L, RF 35mm f/1.8, RF 85mm f/1.2

Noise Reduction Tips:

- In-camera noise reduction works on JPEGs; set to "Low" for balance.
- If shooting RAW, disable NR and apply custom NR in post.
- Use Highlight Tone Priority to reduce clipped bright lights.
- Expose to the right (ETTR): Slightly overexpose and pull down in post to minimize noise in shadows.

Bonus Tip: Enable exposure simulation and histogram in live view to keep exposure accurate in dim conditions.

Final Word: Think Like a Creator, Not Just a Technician

Each of these real-life photo recipes gives you a technical framework—but the real secret to consistently great results lies in how you think about your subject, light, and timing. Once you internalize the setups, you'll be able to tweak on the fly, adapt to chaos, and create with intention—not hesitation.

From weddings to wildlife, street to studio, the Canon R5 Mark II has the tools to elevate your vision.

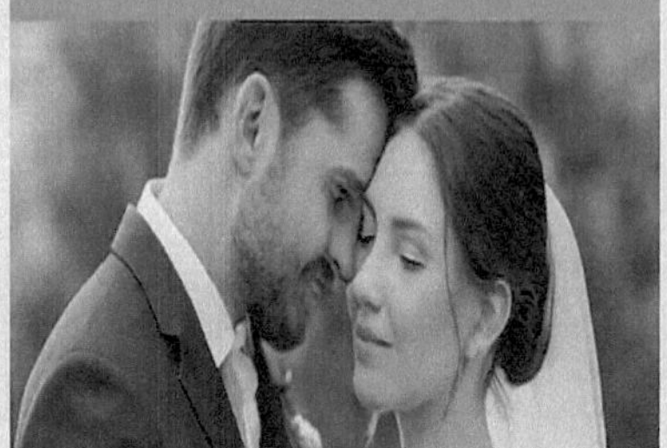

WEDDING SETTINGS FOR SHARP, ROMANTIC IMAGES

Mode: M or Ay
Shutter Speed: 1/200s
Aperture: fi1.8 to /2.8
ISD, Auto (Maz, 6400
WB: AWB (Ambience)
Picture Style: Portrait
AF. Face Have, Servo
Drive: Continuous
Lens: RF 50 mm f/1.2ᒻ

Key Tip: Use back button focus for ceremony

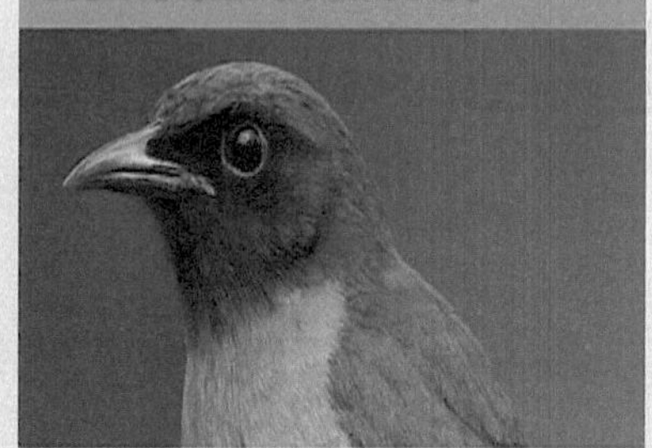

WILDLIFE SETUP WITH EYE-TRACKING FOR BIRDS

Mode: M or Ty
Shutter Speed: 1/600s
Aperture: fi3.8 to I8
ISD, Auto (Maz, 6400
WB: Daylight
Picture Style: Sitandard
AF. Subject: Bird, Whole Area, Servo
Drive: Continuous
Lens: RF 100-500 mm

Key Tip: Assign button for » human detection

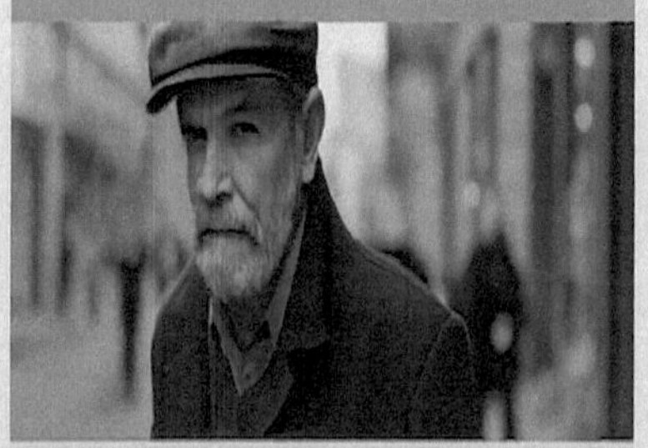

STREET PHOTOGRAPHY SETUP FOR FAST REACTON

Mode: Ay or M
Shutter Speed: 1/500s
Aperture: f/2.2 to f5.6
ISD, Auto
WB: AWB

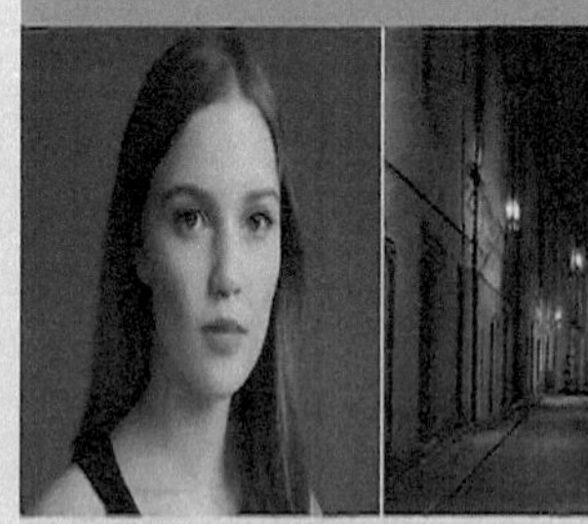

STUDIO PORTRAITS WITH MANUAL FLASH

Mode: M
Shutter Speed: 1/60s to /200s
Aperture: fi1.2 to /2.8
ISD, 2200 g f2800
WB: AWB

Part III: Video Made Simple — 4k, 8k & Cinematic Shooting

Chapter 8:

Video Recording Basics & File Format Clarity

Unlocking the Power of Canon EOS R5 Mark II's Video Beast Mode

If photography is the soul of a camera, video is its heartbeat. And with the Canon EOS R5 Mark II, that heartbeat is cinematic, powerful, and surprisingly intuitive—once you understand what you're looking at.

Canon has pushed the R5 Mark II into true hybrid territory, making it equally comfortable capturing stunning stills or delivering professional-grade 8K RAW footage. But this power comes at the price of complexity. You're suddenly faced with dozens of choices: 8K or 4K HQ? 120fps or 60? Should you shoot All-I or IPB? Can your SD card handle it—or do you need a CFexpress? How do you balance quality, storage, and workflow?

This chapter makes it all simple. No jargon. No guesswork. Just clear explanations and practical tips to help you capture brilliant footage—whether you're vlogging in natural light, shooting a music video, or recording a documentary.

Let's roll.

Understanding All Video Resolutions: 8K RAW, 4K HQ, 4K IPB

The Canon EOS R5 Mark II offers a menu of recording options, each designed to serve a different balance of resolution, bit rate, and post-production flexibility.

8K RAW (8192 x 4320)

- *Best For*: Cinematic filmmaking, post-production flexibility, cropping in post
- *Pros*: Insane detail, RAW flexibility, full-frame readout
- *Cons*: Massive files, generates more heat, requires CFexpress cards
- *File Format*: RAW (.CRM) or RAW Light (.MP4)
- *Post Workflow*: Requires high-end system to edit smoothly; color grading is almost mandatory
- *Storage Demand*: Extremely high

8K gives you unmatched detail, but unless you're working in commercial cinema or doing large-format reframing, it's overkill for most everyday uses.

4K HQ (High Quality)

- *Best For*: Premium YouTube content, weddings, interviews, product videos
- *Pros*: Oversampled from 8K for extra sharpness, beautiful detail
- *Cons*: Higher file sizes than standard 4K, slight crop depending on mode
- *Compression*: Can use All-I or IPB depending on settings
- *Storage Demand*: High but more manageable than 8K

This is the sweet spot for creators who want that "cinematic look" with manageable workflow.

4K IPB (Standard 4K)

- *Best For*: Long-form video, vlogging, client work that doesn't require grading
- *Pros*: Smaller file sizes, easier on memory cards
- *Cons*: Slight drop in sharpness vs 4K HQ
- *Compression*: IPB or Light IPB
- *Storage Demand*: Medium

Most casual users or run-and-gun filmmakers will live here. Still sharp, and with Canon color science, your footage will look great straight out of camera.

Frame Rates: 24, 30, 60, 120fps — and Motion Feel

Choosing the right frame rate influences not just your file size or editing options, but the emotional tone and "feel" of your video.

24fps

- *Best For*: Narrative film, interviews, YouTube talking head
- *Feel*: Cinematic and natural. This is the standard for Hollywood film
- *Notes*: Motion blur is intentional and pleasing

30fps

- *Best For*: Live streaming, corporate videos, weddings
- *Feel*: Crisp and slightly more "video" than 24fps
- *Notes*: Slightly smoother than 24fps—use when you need clarity over style

60fps

- *Best For*: Action scenes, music performances, YouTube b-roll
- *Feel*: Very smooth motion, hyper-real
- *Notes*: Can be conformed to 24fps in editing for slow-motion

120fps (High Frame Rate mode)

- *Best For*: Extreme slow-motion, dance, sports, splash footage
- *Feel*: Ultra-fluid, dreamlike when slowed down
- *Notes*: Audio is not recorded at 120fps, must use background sound/music

Pro Tip: Mixing frame rates is totally okay. Shoot your "A-roll" at 24 or 30fps, and use 60 or 120fps for slow-motion B-roll inserts. Just make sure you conform everything properly in post.

Compression Types: All-I, IPB, and Light IPB

Compression determines how your video data is packed and stored. Think of it as deciding whether to save a suitcase full of clothes neatly folded (All-I) or vacuum-sealed (IPB). Same clothes—different unpacking process.

ALL-I (Intra-frame Compression)

- *Every single frame is compressed individually*
- *Pros*: Easier to edit, higher quality per frame, great for fast-moving scenes
- *Cons*: Bigger files
- *Best For*: Pro editing, action scenes, green screen work

If you want maximum flexibility in post and don't mind larger files, All-I is your best friend.

IPB (Inter-frame Compression)

- *Only changes between frames are recorded*
- *Pros*: Smaller file sizes
- *Cons*: More taxing on your editing system, less ideal for frame-accurate work
- *Best For*: General content creation, vlogging, corporate shoots

IPB Light (Light Inter-frame Compression)

- *Extra compressed for even smaller file size*
- *Pros*: Ideal for long shoots, web content, smaller cards
- *Cons*: Not suited for fast-moving scenes or heavy color correction
- *Best For*: Behind-the-scenes, interviews, casual footage

Rule of Thumb:

- **All-I** if you're editing and color grading
- **IPB** for content that will be lightly edited
- **IPB Light** for long-form capture with limited storage

CFexpress vs SD Card Compatibility for Video

This is where many new users get tripped up. The R5 Mark II has dual card slots:

- **Slot 1**: CFexpress Type B
- **Slot 2**: SD UHS-II

But not all formats are created equal.

CFexpress Type B Cards

- *Required for*: 8K RAW, 4K 120fps, high-bitrate All-I
- *Speed*: 1400–1700 MB/s write speeds
- *Price*: Higher
- *Pros*: Faster, future-proof, better thermal handling
- *Use If*: You're filming professional-grade footage or working in RAW

SD UHS-II Cards

- *Can handle*: 4K IPB, 1080p, still photography, backup recording
- *Speed*: ~300 MB/s max write
- *Price*: More affordable
- *Use If*: You're shooting casual 4K video or using it as a backup slot

Important Caveat:

Some recording modes (like 8K RAW or 4K All-I 60p) won't start if you only insert an SD card. The camera will display a warning and prevent recording. Always check the compatibility chart in the manual or your card specs before important shoots.

Best Practice:

Use a CFexpress card in Slot 1 for video, and an SD card in Slot 2 for proxy recording or stills. Format both before each session to avoid card errors.

Final Word: Film Like a Pro, Without the Guesswork

The Canon R5 Mark II isn't just a stills powerhouse—it's a full-on cinematic machine, capable of delivering footage worthy of festivals, YouTube stardom, or your next brand campaign. But the difference between a frustrating shoot and a fluid one always comes down to understanding formats, settings, and limits.

With this chapter, you now know how to:

- Choose the right resolution for your project
- Set the ideal frame rate for storytelling
- Understand how compression impacts editing and storage
- Pick the right memory cards for your workflow

CHAPTER 8
VIDEO RECORDING BASICS
& FILE FORMAT CLARITY

UNDERSTANDING ALL VIDEO RESOLUTIONS

8K RAW
7680×4320
maximum quality

4K DCI (HQ)
4096×2160
high detail

4K UHD
3840×2160
standard 4K

FULL HD
efiicient file sizes
← 1920×1080 →

FRAME RATES & MOTION STYLES

23.98 or 24 fps
cinematic look

25 or 30 fps
TV, online video

50 or/60 fps
smooth motion

COMPRESSION TYPES EXPLAINED

ALL-I
large file size
best quality
easy to edit

IPB
small file size
good quality
more compression

IPB Light
smaller file size
low bit rate
less quality

CFexpress vs SD CARD FOR VIDEO

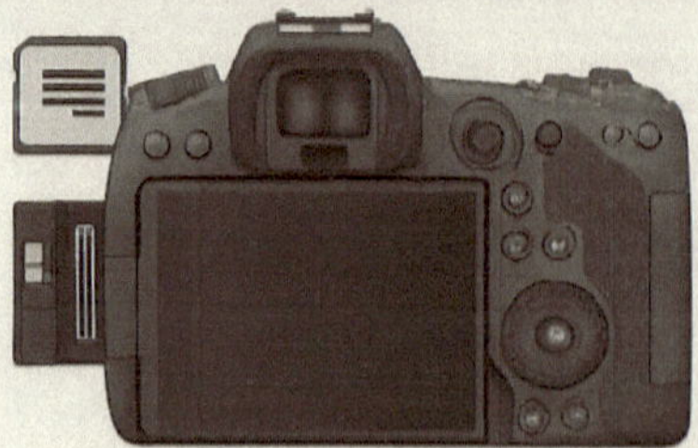
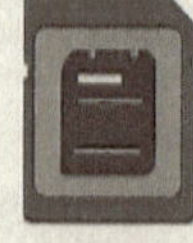

→ requirei for
8K RAW, 4K HQ
→ very fast

→ up to 4K 60/30p
IPB
→ slower

Chapter 9

Heat, Limits & How to Avoid Overheating

Keeping the Canon EOS R5 Mark II Cool Under Pressure

One of the biggest questions surrounding the Canon EOS R5 Mark II—just like its predecessor—is simple but critical: *"Will it overheat?"* The answer is yes—it can. But with the right setup and a few insider strategies, the camera can run cooler, longer, and more reliably than most people expect.

Whether you're recording a 90-minute sit-down interview, filming long-form YouTube content, or capturing live performances, this chapter is your essential guide to understanding the camera's thermal behavior, knowing which modes trigger overheating, and how to extend your record time without compromise.

Because the only thing more frustrating than missing the moment is missing it because your camera overheated.

Let's keep things cool.

What Triggers Overheat Warnings?

The R5 Mark II is significantly improved over the original R5 when it comes to heat management—but it's still a high-performance hybrid machine packed into a compact body. That means heat is a byproduct of power. Here's what you need to understand.

High Heat Triggers:

- 8K Recording, especially RAW or oversampled formats
- 4K 60/120fps in HQ or All-I
- In-body processing during long continuous takes
- Recording in direct sunlight or warm environments
- Using both screens (LCD + EVF) extensively
- Charging via USB-C while recording

Internal Temperature Sensors:

Canon uses internal thermal sensors—not just time-based limits. The camera *monitors actual heat buildup*, and if it crosses certain thresholds, it will:

1. Display a heat warning icon on screen
2. Disable certain formats or frame rates temporarily
3. Automatically shut down recording to cool off

The good news? The R5 Mark II recovers more quickly than the original, and it allows you to monitor temp in real-time so you're not caught off guard.

How to Record Long Videos Without Shutdown

The question every serious user asks is: *Can I record for over an hour straight without crashing the camera?*

Yes—but only if you optimize your setup.

Use These Settings for Long Continuous Recording:

- **Resolution**: 4K IPB or 4K IPB Light (not HQ or All-I)
- **Frame Rate**: 23.98 or 29.97 fps
- **Compression**: IPB or IPB Light
- **Card**: High-speed SD UHS-II (not CFexpress if not needed)
- **Power**: External power (dummy battery or USB PD power bank)
- **Screens**: LCD only, with screen brightness set to "Low"
- **Image Stabilization**: Turn off Digital IS (saves processing heat)
- **Audio**: Record internally or externally—mics don't cause heat

- 8K or 4K HQ (these use full 8K sensor readout)
- 60/120 fps modes
- Constant screen flipping or menu diving
- Recording in direct sun or hot interiors

With this setup, many users report recording 90+ minutes without a single shutdown—especially indoors with ambient cooling.

Cooling Strategies, External Monitors, and C-Log Considerations

To go even further, smart pros employ external gear and settings tricks to pull heat away from the body or reduce internal load.

Passive & Active Cooling Tips:

- **Turn Off the EVF**: Use LCD only or external monitor
- **Use External Monitor**: HDMI out to Atomos Ninja or Feelworld cuts down internal processing
- **Record Externally**: Use the HDMI output to record on an external recorder instead of internally—this removes most of the heavy lifting from the internal system
- **Open Battery Door or Flaps**: When on a rig, letting air flow helps

- **Add a Small Fan**: Even a USB-powered fan blowing near the camera helps more than you think
- **Shade the Camera**: Use a matte box, umbrella, or just avoid direct sunlight
- **Use Dummy Battery with Power Delivery**: This reduces internal battery strain, which contributes to heat

C-Log and Processing Load:

- Shooting in C-Log 3 adds processing load
- If you're not color grading, consider turning off Log and sticking with standard profiles
- If shooting in C-Log, record to CFexpress and use external power to avoid compounding heat

Note: Using C-Log is *not* a direct cause of overheating, but it does keep the processor working harder over time, which can matter in borderline heat conditions.

Real-World Scenario: Best Settings for a 90-Minute Interview

Let's say you're filming a seated documentary interview indoors. The subject is well lit. Audio is handled via lavalier mic into the camera. You want to record the entire session without stopping every 20 minutes.

Here's your ideal setup:

Camera Settings:

- **Resolution**: 4K (Standard), IPB compression
- **Frame Rate**: 29.97 fps
- **Picture Style**: Neutral or Portrait (no Log, since no grading needed)
- **Autofocus**: Eye Detection enabled, Servo AF
- **IBIS**: Off if on tripod
- **Digital IS**: Off
- **Recording to**: SD UHS-II card in slot 2
- **Record Format**: MP4, not RAW
- **Limiters**: Off (set to "Disable Overheat Control Warnings" for confidence, but monitor temp)

Hardware Setup:

- **Power**: Dummy battery connected to AC or USB-C PD power bank
- **Monitoring**: External HDMI monitor for live preview
- **Audio**: Lav mic plugged into 3.5mm input; monitor through headphones
- **Lighting**: Continuous LED softbox (cool running)

Environmental Setup:

- **Temperature**: Air-conditioned room or fan-cooled
- **Camera Position**: Shaded from key light

- **Ventilation**: Keep side doors (card/battery) ajar if possible

This rig allows most users to shoot for 90–120 minutes without interruption, even with the LCD flipped for monitoring.

Final Word: Mastering Heat is Mastering Confidence

Heat shouldn't be a mystery—it should be a metric you manage. Once you understand what triggers the Canon R5 Mark II to warm up, and how to cool it back down or avoid pushing its limits in the first place, you'll be free to focus on the content—not the countdown clock.

With a few practical tools, a mindful workflow, and the right video settings, you can shoot weddings, interviews, events, and even long-format YouTube videos without missing a beat.

HEAT, LIMITS & HOW TO AVOID OVERHEATING

WHAT TRIGGERS OVERHEAT WARNINGS

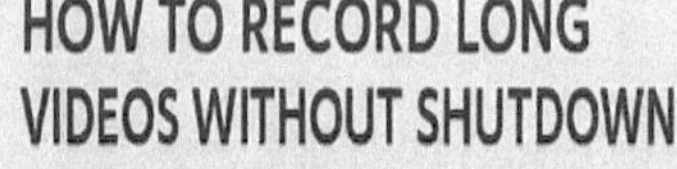

- 8K OR 4K 60/120 FPS VIDEO
- DIRECT SUNLIGHT SHOOTING
- DUAL SCREEN USE
- USB-C CHARGING WHILE RECORDING
- INTERNAL HEAT SENSORS DETECT

HOW TO RECORD LONG VIDEOS WITHOUT SHUTDOWN

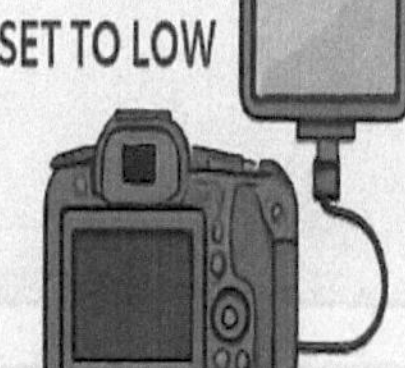

- 4K 24/30 FPS OR IPB LIGHT
- SD CARD INSTEAD OF CEEXPRESS
- EXTERNAL POWER SOURCE
- DISABLE IBIS & DIGITAL IS
- LCD SCREEN SET TO LOW

COOLING STRATEGIES EXTERNAL MONITOR, AND C-LOG CONSIDERATIONS

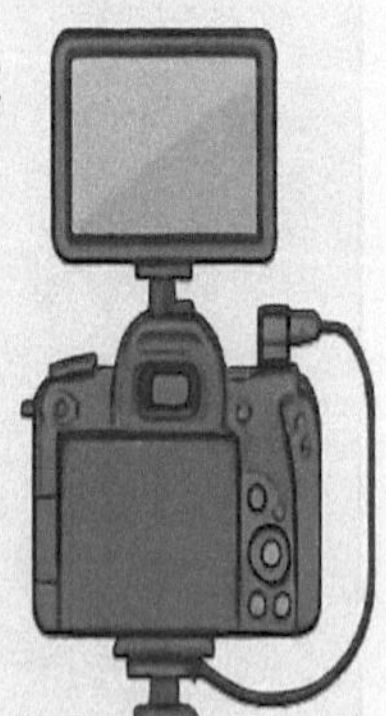

- TURN OFF EVF OR USE HDMI OUT
- ADD MONITOR BRIGHTNESS TO REDUCE HEAT
- CONSIDER IF C-LOG IS NEEDED

REAL-WORLD SCENARIO: BEST SETTINGS FOR A 90-MINUTE INTERVIEW

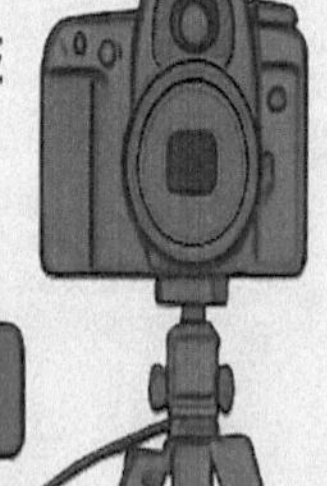

- 4K 24 FPS, IPB COMPRESSION
- IBIS & EVF DISABLED
- NEUTRAL PICTURE STYLE
- DUMMY BATTERY POWERING

Chapter 10

Mastering Canon Log, H.265 & Post Workflow

Elevate Your Footage from Good to Cinematic

If there's one chapter where image science meets storytelling power, this is it. Canon Log, 10-bit color, and H.265 compression might sound like intimidating terms—but they hold the keys to unlocking footage that breathes, pops, and tells a story with color, mood, and texture.

The Canon EOS R5 Mark II isn't just capable of recording beautiful images—it's engineered for filmmakers and hybrid shooters who want their footage to stand up in post-production. Whether you're matching your R5 II with a second camera, color grading for a short film, or building cinematic LUTs for YouTube, you'll want to understand how Log profiles, bit depth, and codecs interact.

This chapter demystifies all of it—from what Canon Log 3 actually does, to why your editing software might choke on H.265 unless you know the trick. No fluff. No unnecessary jargon. Just a clean breakdown of how to shoot for post, and how to make your editing life easier (and more powerful) as a result.

When and Why to Use Canon Log 3

Canon Log 3 (C-Log 3) is a gamma curve designed to capture a wider dynamic range, allowing you to retain detail in both the shadows and highlights—ideal for scenes with tricky lighting or where flexibility in post is key.

Use Canon Log 3 When:

- You're shooting scenes with strong contrast (e.g., backlighting, sunsets, interiors with bright windows)
- You plan to color grade in post-production
- You want to match footage from other Canon cinema cameras (like C70, C300)
- You're building a LUT-based workflow

Avoid Canon Log 3 When:

- You don't plan to color grade
- You need quick delivery without much editing
- You want rich contrast straight out of camera (use Neutral or Portrait profiles instead)

C-Log 3 gives a flatter, low-contrast look in-camera—but that's intentional. It preserves data. When color graded, it gives you smoother skin tones, better highlight roll-off, and cinematic control.

10-Bit vs 8-Bit: What It Means in Color Grading

Let's simplify bit depth:

- **8-bit video** records 256 shades per channel (red, green, blue)
- **10-bit video** records 1,024 shades per channel

This might not seem huge on paper—but it's massive in post. It means:

- No banding in gradients (sunsets, skies, skin)
- More precise color grading without artifacts
- Better performance when applying LUTs or corrections

Most mirrorless cameras used to be limited to 8-bit internal recording. The R5 Mark II records 10-bit 4:2:2 internally—meaning you get high color fidelity and data-rich footage right out of the box.

Use 10-bit:

- For any Log shooting
- When mixing cameras or building LUTs
- For pro delivery (ads, music videos, narrative)

- For casual YouTube, social media, or quick-turn projects
- When storage or editing speed is limited

One thing to note: 10-bit files are larger and more processor-intensive. Make sure your editing software (and hardware) can handle them smoothly.

Best Codecs for Editing in Premiere Pro, DaVinci, or Final Cut

Canon's R5 Mark II records in modern, high-efficiency formats—great for storage, but sometimes a challenge in post if your system isn't optimized.

Common Recording Codecs:

- **H.265 (HEVC)**: Efficient but heavy to edit. Great for delivery, tougher in timeline playback.
- **H.264**: Lighter than H.265, more universally supported
- **RAW or RAW Light**: Incredibly flexible, but requires strong hardware and large storage
- **ALL-I vs IPB**: ALL-I is easier to edit, IPB is more compressed (lighter to store)

Best Practice for Each NLE:

Premiere Pro

- Use H.265 with proxies, or transcode to ProRes LT for smoother editing
- For 10-bit H.265, make sure you enable hardware acceleration (Intel Quick Sync or Nvidia CUDA)
- Use Lumetri panel with LUTs to grade Canon Log 3 footage

DaVinci Resolve

- Excellent H.265 support—optimized for Log workflows
- Use the Color Management system for Canon Wide Gamut to Rec.709 conversions
- If your system lags, transcode to DNxHR or ProRes for smoother editing

Final Cut Pro X

- Works well with 10-bit H.265
- Use Camera LUTs to convert C-Log 3 to Rec.709
- Create optimized media in ProRes for heavy projects

General Tip:

If you shoot in C-Log 3 + 10-bit, and your editing timeline stutters or lags, transcoding to ProRes 422 or ProRes LT is the best solution. You'll retain quality, reduce playback lag, and simplify your grade.

Color Matching Tips for Hybrid Shooters

If you're shooting both stills and video, or using multiple cameras (like a Canon C70 and an R5 II), color matching can be tricky—but it's totally doable with a few smart workflows.

Tips for Consistent Color:

- Use Canon Log 3 on all Canon cameras where available
- Set all cameras to Canon Wide Gamut color space
- Use the same white balance setting (don't mix auto WB and presets)
- Avoid Picture Styles like Portrait or Landscape if shooting video—these bake in contrast
- Use color checkers (like X-Rite ColorChecker Video) in the frame to calibrate color in post
- Apply the same conversion LUT (e.g., C-Log 3 to Rec.709) to all footage
- For stills, shoot in RAW and apply similar grading in Lightroom to match the tone of your video

Hybrid shooters often struggle with the disconnect between punchy JPEG stills and flat Log video. The solution? Match the tone in post—not in camera. Shoot both in RAW (stills) and Log (video), and build a cohesive visual story with consistent shadows, skin tones, and highlights.

Final Word: You Don't Need to Be a Colorist to Create Beautiful Video

The Canon R5 Mark II offers more than just beautiful footage—it offers control. But to unlock that control, you need to understand the language of post: what Log does, how bit depth matters, and how codecs affect your workflow.

You now know:

- When to shoot in C-Log 3
- Why 10-bit recording changes the game
- Which editing apps and formats will serve you best
- How to build consistency in hybrid projects

Whether you're filming a documentary, vlogging a travel series, or building content for clients, the R5 II delivers pro-level video—if you know how to shape it.

And now you do.

MASTERING CANON LOG, H .265 & POST WORKFLOW

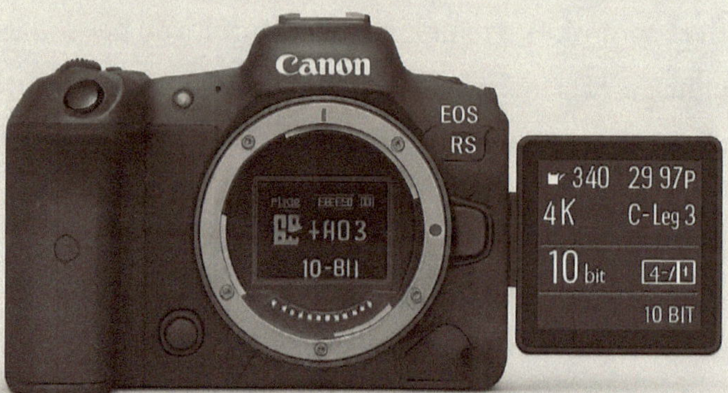

WHEN TO USE CANON LOG 3

MORE DYNAMIC RANGE

COLOR GRADING FLEXIBILITY

MATCHING OTHER CAMERAS

DON'T USE
(IF QUICK TURNAROUND NEEDED)

10-BIT VS 8-BIT

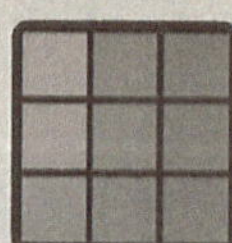

10-BIT   8-BIT

10-BIT ALLOWS FOR SMOOTHER GRADIENTS

BEST CODECS FOR EDITING

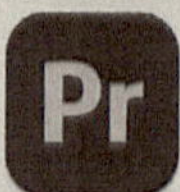

H.264
LIGHT
EDITING

PRORES
SMOOTH
EDITING

MAKE
PROXIES
FOR H.265

COLOR MATCHING TIPS

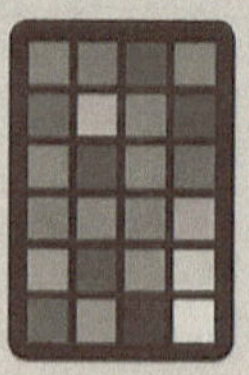

USE SAME WHITE BALANCE

REFERENCE A COLOR CHART

- CONVERT LOG TO REC. 709

Chapter 11

Cinematic Video Recipes

Your Step-by-Step Guide to Visual Storytelling with the Canon EOS R5 Mark II

You've explored the menus. Mastered autofocus. Learned how to shoot in Log, decode compression types, and manage overheating. Now it's time to put all of that to work and craft footage that feels cinematic—not just technically correct, but emotionally resonant.

In this chapter, we move beyond settings and into scenes. These cinematic video recipes are real-world, repeatable setups designed to help you shoot stunning footage whether you're filming a short film, a wedding highlight, a music video, or moody travel content.

Each setup walks you through lens choice, camera settings, picture profile, stabilization method, audio tips, lighting advice, and composition strategies—so you can recreate that big-screen look with the gear you already have.

1. Short Film Setup: Narrative Scene with

Dialogue

Scene Description: Two characters in conversation under soft daylight in a living room or park.

Camera Setup:

- **Resolution**: 4K HQ (Full sensor readout for cinematic depth)
- **Frame Rate**: 23.98 fps
- **Compression**: All-I
- **Picture Profile**: Canon Log 3 + 10-bit
- **White Balance**: Custom set (using grey card)
- **Stabilization**: Tripod or gimbal for movement
- **Lenses**: 35mm f/1.4 or 50mm f/1.2 for shallow DOF
- **Focus Mode**: Eye Detection AF (one-shot if actors are seated)

Audio:

- External shotgun mic on boom pole
- Record externally and sync in post (use clap or timecode)

Lighting:

- Diffused daylight or LED panels with softboxes
- Use practical lights (lamps) for warm accents

Tips:

- Block the scene before rolling—know your cuts.
- Let highlights clip naturally in backgrounds (e.g., windows).
- Shoot close-ups at f/2 to isolate emotion.

2. Travel Sequence: Golden Hour B-Roll

Scene Description: Solo subject walking through a coastal town during sunset.

Camera Setup:

- **Resolution**: 4K Standard
- **Frame Rate**: 60 fps (for slow motion in post)
- **Compression**: IPB Light
- **Picture Profile**: Neutral or C-Log 3 with baked-in LUT
- **White Balance**: Daylight fixed (to retain warmth)
- **Stabilization**: IBIS + Digital IS On
- **Lenses**: 24-70mm f/2.8 or 35mm prime
- **Focus Mode**: Face + Eye Detect AF, Servo

Audio:

- Ambient sound only—record external foley later

Lighting:

- Natural light only; shoot during golden hour

Tips:

- Pan slowly with the subject to retain softness.
- Use foreground elements (walls, trees) for depth.
- Don't overexpose the sky—use exposure compensation.

3. Wedding Highlight: Bride Walk-In Scene

Scene Description: The bride walks down the aisle, slow motion, emotion-packed.

Camera Setup:

- **Resolution**: 4K 60fps
- **Frame Rate**: 60 fps (slow to 24 in post)
- **Compression**: All-I
- **Picture Profile**: C-Log 3 with LUT applied
- **White Balance**: Kelvin set to match venue (around 4500K)
- **Stabilization**: Gimbal or monopod
- **Lenses**: 85mm f/1.2 or 70-200mm f/2.8
- **Focus Mode**: Face tracking with custom sensitivity

Audio:

- Capture ambient crowd noise on separate mic
- Ceremony audio on lavs—cut away from this moment

Lighting:

- Use available lighting; raise shadows in post

Tips:

- Don't chase—pre-anticipate the movement.
- Frame for headroom and veil flow.
- Shoot multiple takes from different angles if possible.

4. Music Video: Artist Performance Scene

Scene Description: Artist performing to camera with colored lighting and expressive movement.

Camera Setup:

- **Resolution**: 8K RAW Light (if you want maximum crop-in flexibility)
- **Frame Rate**: 24 fps
- **Picture Profile**: Canon Log 3, Wide Gamut
- **White Balance**: Manual match to gels
- **Stabilization**: Gimbal or slider
- **Lenses**: 16-35mm f/2.8 or 24mm f/1.4
- **Focus Mode**: Manual focus or AF lock for consistency

Audio:

- Track playback synced externally
- Focus on visual sync only

Lighting:

- Colored LED panels
- Use smoke or haze for atmosphere

Tips:

- Shoot handheld for raw energy.
- Mix close-ups with wide silhouettes.
- Use whip pans and zooms to create energy transitions.

5. Night Walk & Talk: Urban Cinematic Vibes

Scene Description: Couple walking under neon signs, naturalistic dialogue, shallow DOF.

Camera Setup:

- **Resolution**: 4K All-I
- **Frame Rate**: 24 fps
- **Picture Profile**: C-Log 3, Noise Reduction Low
- **White Balance**: 3200K or match streetlights
- **Stabilization**: IBIS only or handheld with cage
- **Lenses**: 35mm f/1.4 or 50mm f/1.2
- **Focus Mode**: Servo AF, Face Detect with Tracking

Audio:

- Lavalier mics (if capturing sync dialogue)
- Use external recorder for cleaner sound

Lighting:

- Use available signage + handheld LED fill

Tips:

- Let shadows stay dark—preserve mood.
- Use traffic light changes for creative transitions.
- Be mindful of ISO—don't go past 6400 if you want clean skin.

Final Thoughts: Cinematic Is a Feeling, Not Just a Format

You now have a creative blueprint for turning your Canon R5 Mark II into a cinematic storytelling machine.

Remember, cinematic doesn't mean expensive or complex. It means intentionality—in your lighting, framing, movement, and emotion.

Each of these recipes is a tool, not a rule. Use them as springboards. Combine elements. Adapt the techniques to your own story. Film is an emotional language—and you now speak it fluently through this camera.

CHAPTER 11
CINEMATIC VIDEO RECIPES

🎬 SHORT FILM SETUP

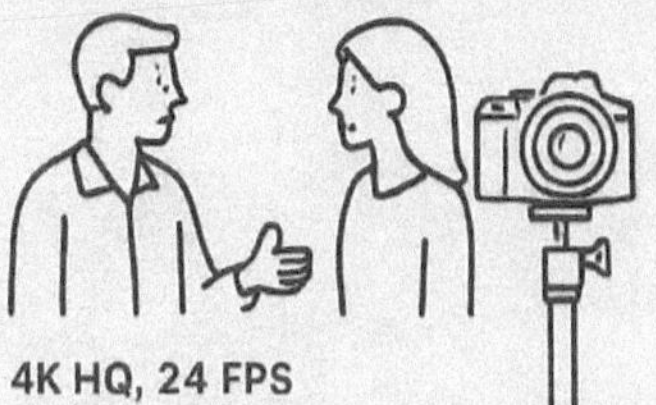

4K HQ, 24 FPS
LOG: C-LOG 3
STABILIZATION: TRIPOD
LENS: 35MM F/1.4

⛰ TRAVEL SEQUENCE

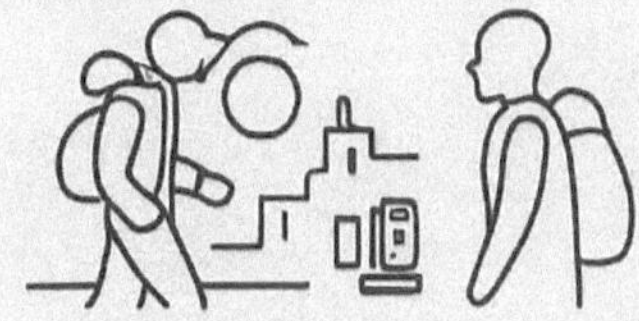

4K. 60 FPS
LOG: NEUTRAL +LUT
STABILIZATION: IBIS +DIGITAL IS
LENS: 24-70MM F/2.8

⬡ WEDDING HIGHLIGHT

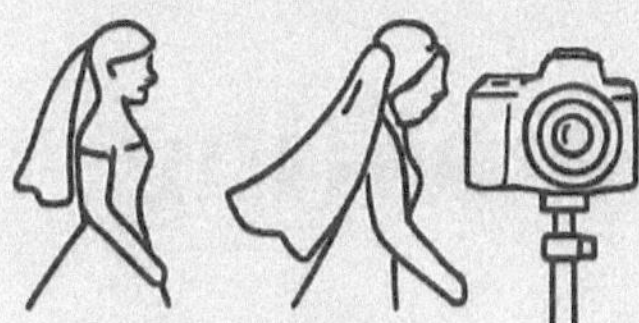

4K. 60 FPS (SLOMO)
LOG: C-LOG 3 + LUT
STABILIZATION: GIMBAL
LENS: 85MM F/1.2

🎤 MUSIC VIDEO

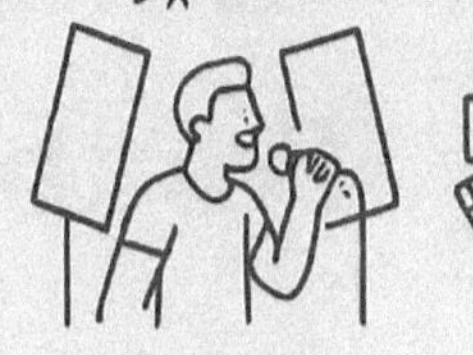

8K RAW. 24 FPS
LOG: C-LOG 3
STABILIZATION: GIMBAL
LENS: 24MM F/1.4

🌙 NIGHT WALK & TALK

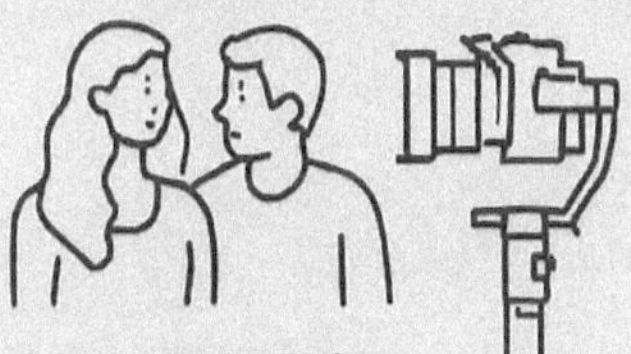

4K ALL-1, 24 FPS
LOG: C-LOG 3
STABILIZATION: IANDHELD (CAGE)
LENS: 50MM F/1.2

👕 NI H WALK & TALK

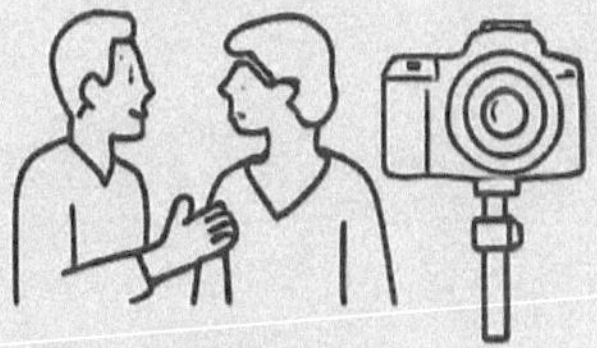

4K ALL-1, 24 FPS
LOG: C-LOG 3
STABILIZATION: HANDHELD (CAGE)
LENS: 50MM F/1.2

Part IV: Advanced Functions & Troubleshooting

Chapter 12

Image Stabilization (IBIS) — Blessing or Burden?

Understanding When Canon's Stabilization Helps... and When It Hurts

Image stabilization on modern mirrorless cameras is often praised as a game-changer—and for good reason. Canon's In-Body Image Stabilization (IBIS) on the EOS R5 Mark II can deliver stunningly smooth handheld footage and tack-sharp images at slow shutter speeds. But it's not always the magic bullet creators expect. Especially when paired with certain wide-angle lenses or used in motion-heavy shooting, it can introduce odd distortions, sometimes referred to as "IBIS wobble" or "jello."

So is Canon's IBIS a creative friend or a technical foe?

In this chapter, we'll break down how IBIS actually works in the R5 II, why it can sometimes interfere with lens stabilization (IS), what causes those strange edge distortions in wide-angle video—and how to avoid all of it with practical, real-world setups.

Whether you're shooting handheld B-roll, vlogging on the street, or capturing low-light photos at 1/5s, you'll leave this chapter knowing when to trust IBIS and when to rein it in.

How Canon IBIS Works

Canon's In-Body Image Stabilization (IBIS) is built into the camera sensor itself. It physically shifts the sensor to counteract small hand movements in five axes: pitch, yaw, roll, horizontal shift, and vertical shift. This happens in real time—thousands of micro-adjustments per second.

When paired with Canon's optical Image Stabilization (IS) in lenses, especially RF glass, the two systems work together. This is called coordinated IS, and it allows for up to 8 stops of stabilization in certain combinations.

That means:

- You can handhold a shot at 1/4s and still get sharp results.
- Your handheld video feels more gimbal-like—if used right.

But...

When IBIS and Lens IS Clash

Not all stabilization systems play nicely. And while Canon has made huge improvements in firmware and coordination algorithms, there are situations where IBIS and lens IS can fight each other rather than cooperate.

This happens most often with:

- Wide-angle lenses (15–35mm range)
- Slow, handheld pans
- Tripod shots with IS left on
- Third-party lenses that don't fully communicate with Canon's IS system

The result? You might see:

- **Wobbly or "warped" edges** in video
- A **jittery drift** when you're trying to pan smoothly
- **Unnatural-looking stabilization pulses** in the center of the frame

This is especially frustrating when you're shooting slow, artistic B-roll and expecting smoothness—but get jello instead.

How to Avoid the Wobble with Wide-Angles

To avoid these issues without giving up stabilization completely, use these tips:

Use Digital IS Only When Needed

Canon gives you three levels of video stabilization:

- IBIS (hardware only)
- IS (lens-based)
- Digital IS (software-based, adds slight crop)

Turn off Digital IS if you're seeing warp. It's the most aggressive and often overcorrects.

Use a Gimbal for Motion

If you're moving a lot (walk-and-talks, parallax moves), disable all in-camera stabilization and rely on a gimbal. Let the mechanical system do the work.

For Static or Tripod Shots: Turn IS Off

Both IBIS and lens IS can create unnecessary micro-adjustments when the camera is actually still. This introduces jitter, not smoothness.

If you're shooting video at 15mm or wider, consider turning IBIS off and using manual stability techniques like:

- Holding with two hands
- Using a strap to anchor the body
- Leaning against a wall or using a monopod

Use Lenses with Coordinated IS (e.g., RF 24-105mm f/4L)

These lenses are designed to work in harmony with IBIS and produce the best results, especially in hybrid photography + video workflows.

Stabilization Best Practices for Handheld Video

For smooth, natural footage without artifacts, these field-tested techniques work best:

1. Keep Your Movements Intentional

IBIS corrects for minor tremors, not big motions. Don't let it "fight" your movement—move slowly and with purpose.

2. Use Slow Shutter Speeds in Moderation

In low light, it's tempting to drop to 1/25s or lower. That's okay for static handheld shots, but adds motion blur in video. Stick to 1/50–1/125s for most handheld footage.

3. Balance Your Camera Setup

A lightweight camera with a heavy lens is harder to stabilize. Use smallrig cages or add a top handle for better balance and two-point contact.

4. Layer Stabilization in Post

If your shot is only slightly off, use post-stabilization in Premiere Pro (Warp Stabilizer), DaVinci Resolve (Stabilizer tab), or Final Cut Pro. But don't rely on it too heavily—it can warp footage when pushed.

5. Use Canon's Digital IS Sparingly

Great for emergencies or extreme handheld zooms—but it crops and can introduce noise. Test before committing.

Final Take: Know When to Trust IBIS—and When to Take the Wheel

Canon's IBIS system on the R5 Mark II is a powerful ally when used wisely. It shines in stills, portraiture, slow handheld pans, and light walk-and-talks. But when you push it into ultra-wide territory or forget to disable it on a tripod, it can introduce subtle—but frustrating—problems.

The key is knowing when to use it, when to trust your hands, and when to bring in the right tool (like a gimbal). You're not just capturing stable footage—you're crafting motion that feels cinematic, confident, and clear.

And now you know how to make that decision every time.

CHAPTER 12: IMAGE STABILIZATION (IBIS) — BLESSING OR BURDEN?

How Canon IBIS Works

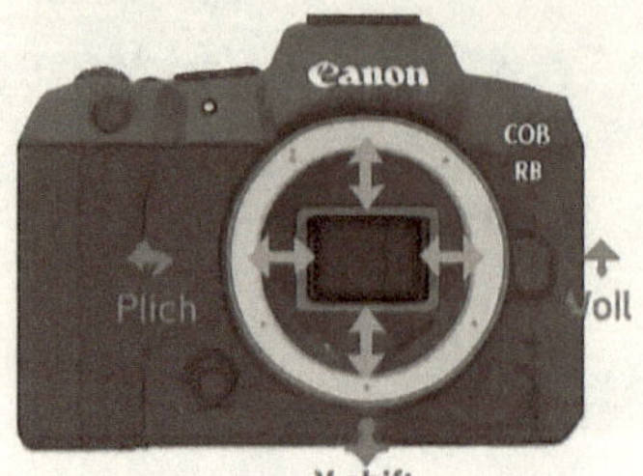

The sensor moves to correct camera motion, working together with stabilized lenses

When IBIS and Lens IS Clash

May cause jello-like distortion with:

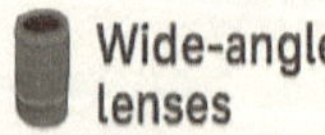

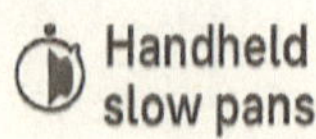

- Wide-angle lenses
- Handheld slow pans

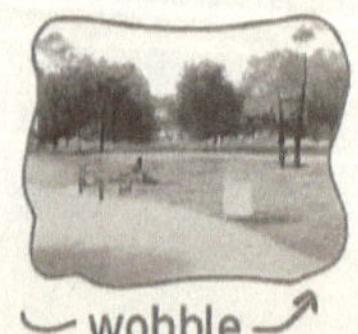

When IBIS and Lens IS Clash

May cause jello-like distortion with:

- Wide-angle lenses
- Handheld slow pans

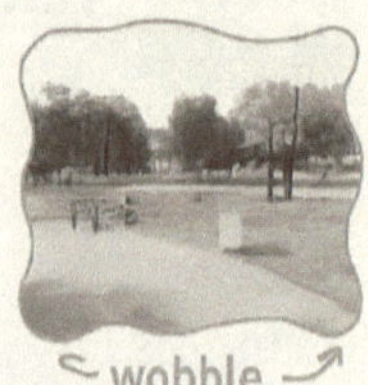

How to Avoid the Wobble with Wide-Angles

Consider turning off I3 for smoother panning

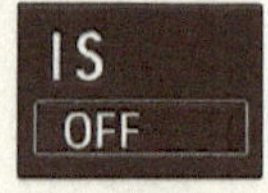

Use a gimbal or cage for added stability

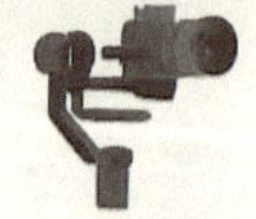

Hold the camera steady, especialy at 15mm or wider

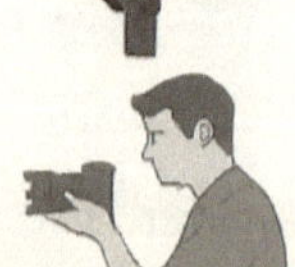

Stabilization Best Practices for Handheld Video

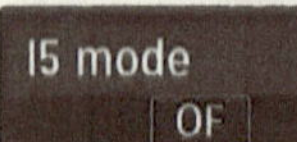

Can subtly reduce shake but adds crop

Use F2.1 dirvo sizing

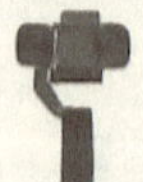
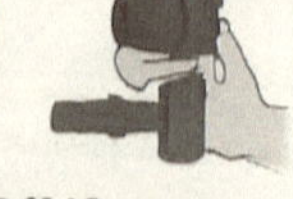

Turn Off IS for tripod or static scenes

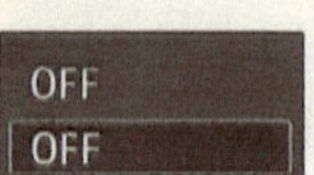

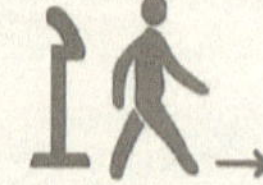

Avoid Excess Motion Walk slowly, use careful movements

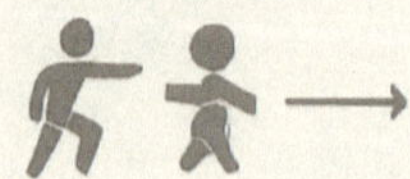

Chapter 13

Battery, Power, and USB-C Recording

Keeping the Canon EOS R5 Mark II Running Without Interruption

One of the most common frustrations for Canon R5 Mark II users—especially video shooters—is battery life. You've got this beast of a camera that can shoot 8K RAW, run high-speed autofocus, power in-body stabilization, and record long-form video sessions. But all that power comes at a cost: battery consumption is *ruthless*.

In this chapter, we're going to tackle the energy-hungry nature of the R5 Mark II and teach you how to tame it—whether you're shooting an all-day wedding, livestreaming for two hours, or just recording casual content without running out of juice mid-take.

We'll also dive into USB-C power delivery, dummy battery systems, and external monitoring, including how to keep everything running cool, efficient, and uninterrupted.

Why the R5 Mark II Drains Batteries Fast

Canon's LP-E6NH battery is powerful—but not magical. And with the R5 Mark II, you're pushing every boundary of mirrorless camera engineering.

Here's why you'll see battery bars drop quicker than expected:

- **8K RAW & 4K HQ modes** use massive processing power.
- **IBIS + Digital IS + Lens IS** draws additional current.
- **AF tracking with AI subjects** keeps processors active.
- **Dual card writing** (especially to CFexpress) taxes system resources.
- **Bright LCD or EVF preview** in high frame rates increases draw.

It's not just about shooting—idle preview, menu navigation, and heat management all contribute to rapid drain.

Bottom line: if you're relying on a single battery for an all-day shoot, you're going to hit a wall.

The Smart Shooter's Power Arsenal

If you're serious about video, livestreaming, or long photo sessions, here's how to power the R5 Mark II like a pro:

1. Extra LP-E6NH Batteries (Official Canon or High-Quality Third Party)

- Always carry at least 2–3 spares for a full day.
- Use the newer LP-E6NH for full compatibility and longer life.
- Be cautious with cheap knockoffs—they may not support USB-C pass-through or may trigger warning messages.

2. Dummy Battery + DC Adapter

This is the gold standard for studio use or any static shooting scenario.

- A dummy battery fits into your battery compartment and is powered via wall outlet or power bank.
- Canon's DR-E6C + CA-PS700 AC adapter is the official combo.
- This allows unlimited runtime without overheating.

Perfect for:

- Long interviews
- Product videos
- YouTube setups
- Live streaming sessions

3. USB-C Power Delivery (PD) Power Banks

Canon R5 Mark II supports USB Power Delivery (PD) input through its USB-C port. But there are some limitations and quirks to understand:

- The USB-C port can power the camera or charge the battery—but not both at the same time during intense use.
- If you're recording high-bitrate video or writing to dual cards, the camera may still draw more power than it's receiving.
- You need a PD-certified power bank (like Anker, Zendure, or OmniCharge) that delivers 9V/3A or 15V/2A minimum.

Pro Tip: For uninterrupted shooting, keep the battery inside the camera even when using USB-C power. It helps balance draw spikes and prevents sudden shutdowns.

4. Live Streaming Setup (with Power Stability)

Live streaming on the R5 Mark II can be done via:

- Clean HDMI out to a capture card (Elgato CamLink 4K, ATEM Mini)
- USB-C direct webcam streaming mode

Regardless of which method you choose:

- Use dummy power if your stream is longer than 45 minutes.

- Turn off unnecessary features like IBIS and auto previews to reduce drain.

- Lower screen brightness and set the EVF to off when not in use.

Recording to External Monitors (Atomos Ninja, etc.)

Recording externally gives you higher-quality ProRes files, less strain on internal cards, and slightly reduced heat. But it also adds power requirements.

If you're using something like the Atomos Ninja V+ to capture 8K or high-bitrate 4K:

- Power the monitor separately (don't drain the R5 battery with it).

- Use a dummy battery for the R5 or a USB-C power bank to ensure both devices stay running.

- Avoid hot-swapping batteries on the monitor—it may disrupt signal or corrupt footage.

Best Practices for Long Video Shoots

Whether you're shooting a podcast, wedding ceremony, music video, or documentary interview, here are the golden rules for power and stability:

Pre-shoot Checklist:

- Format your cards
- Fully charge all batteries (camera + audio + monitor)
- Mount dummy battery if indoors
- Set EVF and LCD to minimal brightness

During Shooting:

- Use record timers or on-screen overlays to monitor runtime
- Periodically check internal temperature
- Stick to standard 4K IPB or All-I 4K for long takes—avoid 8K unless necessary

For Safety:

- Always keep at least one spare LP-E6NH battery ready
- Use high-endurance CFexpress cards for long recordings to avoid corruption
- Test your entire power setup before going live or rolling

Final Thought: Stable Power = Creative Freedom

It's easy to overlook battery management—until the camera dies 3 minutes before the bride walks in or mid-way through your live workshop.

By understanding your Canon R5 Mark II's power demands, investing in smart accessories, and mastering power delivery setups, you'll never be caught off-guard again. The camera can only create what you allow it to. So give it the juice it needs—and let your creative sessions run free, uninterrupted.

CHAPTER 13: BATTERY, POWER, AND USB-C RECORDING

Heavy features like 8K, Dual Pixel AF, and IBIS/IS drain batteries fast. Learn which power options work for long shoots, live streaming, external monitors, and long recording sessions.

🔋 WHY R5 MARK II DRAINS BATTERIES FAST

- 8K video capture
- In-body (IBIS) + lens stabilization
- High-performance subject tracking
- IM (IBIS) + lens stabilization
- Writing to dual memory cards
- Heat management

THE SMART SHOOTER'S POWER ARSENAL

Extra LP-E6NH Batteries

- Use Canon or high-quality third-party batteries
- Carry multiple charged spares

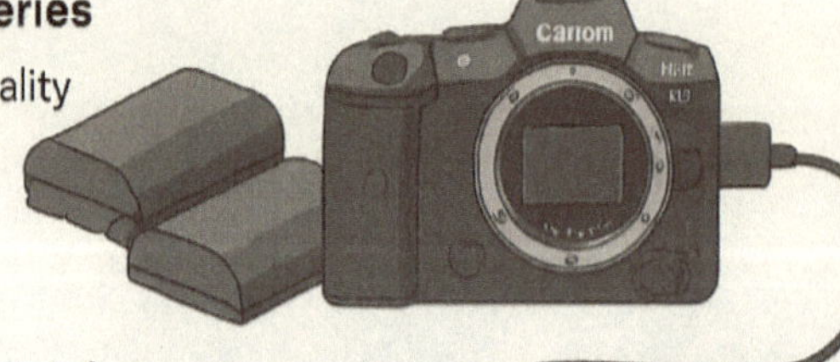

Dummy Battery + DC Adapter

- Use dummy battery & power adapter for long shooting sessions
- Use a PD powerbank for long-and-gun video

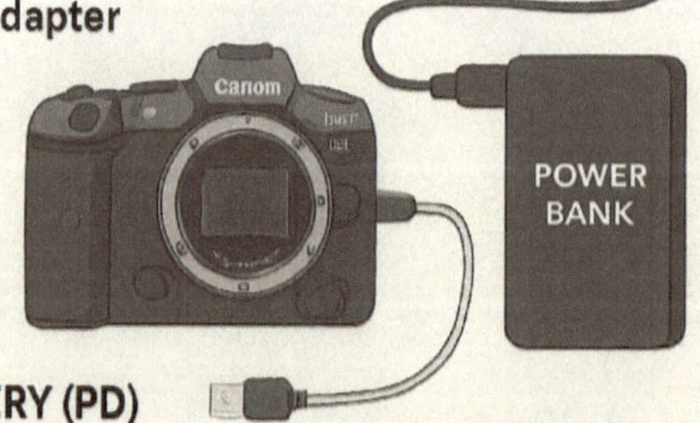

USB-C POWER DELIVERY (PD)

- ⚡ Use dummy battery for stable power When streaming or recording
- Record extemally for long & expand heat times

⚡ LIVE STREAMING, EXTERNAL MONITORS

- Use dummy battery for siable poner
- Long sessions or record long sess
- Record externally for duration heat

Chapter 14

Memory Card Mastery — CFexpress vs SD

How to Choose, Use, and Protect Your Footage Like a Pro

Your Canon EOS R5 Mark II is a performance monster. It shoots 8K RAW, 4K at 120fps, ultra-fast bursts, and high-bitrate log footage. But none of that matters if your memory card can't keep up—or worse, corrupts mid-shoot.

In this chapter, you'll learn how to choose the right memory card for your shooting style, what happens when you mix CFexpress and SD, and the golden rules for formatting, recording, and recovering files when things go wrong.

The R5 Mark II has two card slots: one for CFexpress Type B, and the other for UHS-II SD cards. Each has its strengths. But understanding their limits—and how to use them together—is the key to smooth, stress-free shooting.

What Each Card Type Can Handle

CFexpress Type B

- **Blazing fast**: Up to 1700MB/s read, 1400MB/s write
- **Required** for:
  - 8K RAW
  - 4K 120fps ALL-I
  - High-speed burst (RAW + JPEG)
- **Ideal for**:
  - ProRes external workflows
  - Wedding/event shooters who can't risk dropped frames

CFexpress is your go-to card when performance is non-negotiable.

▯ SD UHS-II (V90 Recommended)

- **Slower**: 300MB/s peak read, ~260MB/s write
- **Works for**:
  - 4K IPB (Standard/Light)
  - 1080p video
  - Photography (JPEG, standard RAW)
- **Not recommended for**:
  - 8K
  - 10-bit log video

- Dual recording of large files

Use SD cards for lighter workloads or as a backup when redundancy matters more than speed.

Mixing CFexpress and SD: What Happens?

The R5 Mark II allows simultaneous recording to both card slots—but only at the speed of the slowest card. This means:

- If you try to record 8K RAW and set the camera to mirror the file to an SD card, it won't work—the SD card can't handle the bitrate.
- If you use CFexpress for video and SD for stills, you're safe—as long as you assign them correctly in the Record Function + Card/folder settings.

Key rule: Never mix high-bitrate files across slow and fast cards. It will either drop frames, stop recording, or disable certain modes entirely.

Best Practices for Formatting, Dual Slot

Recording, and Recovery

Always Format In-Camera

Formatting your cards inside the R5 Mark II:

- Optimizes the file system for Canon's buffer and codec structure
- Clears hidden temporary files from previous sessions
- Reduces chances of file system errors

Avoid formatting on your computer unless absolutely necessary.

Use the Right Format Type

- Use exFAT for cards over 32GB (modern cards default to this).
- Avoid FAT32 if possible—it limits file sizes and fragments large videos.

Dual Slot Recording Modes

In your menu under Shooting Functions > Record func+card/folder sel., you can choose:

- **Standard**: Use one card until it's full, then switch
- **Auto Switch**: Automatically jumps to second card

- **Simultaneous Recording**: Write identical files to both cards (for backup)
- **RAW/JPEG Split**: Write RAW to one, JPEG to the other
- **Video/Photo Split**: Separate stills and video by card

Pro tip: For weddings or corporate work, use Simultaneous mode for maximum safety. Losing footage is not an option.

Monitor Write Speed Icons

If your SD card is too slow, Canon will show:

- **Buffer warning** during burst
- **Recording disabled** for certain video modes
- **"Slow Card" warning** with playback lag

If you see these, upgrade your card or use a different format.

Recovery Tips: When Things Go Wrong

Memory cards are tiny vaults. If something corrupts or fails, don't panic—here's what to do:

Stop Using the Card

Don't reformat. Don't record again. This can overwrite recoverable data.

Use Recovery Software

Tools like PhotoRec, Disk Drill, or Stellar Photo Recovery can pull footage from a damaged card—especially if files were deleted or the card wasn't formatted.

Use a High-Speed Card Reader

Slow readers can fail to mount CFexpress cards properly. Get a USB 3.1 reader rated for your card speed.

Pro Safety Tip:

If you're shooting mission-critical video (like interviews or events), rotate cards every few hours and offload footage to a laptop or SSD as you go. Redundancy isn't optional—it's a professional habit.

Final Word: Cards Can Be Your Weakest Link or Strongest Ally

The Canon EOS R5 Mark II pushes boundaries—but only as far as your memory can handle. CFexpress gives you freedom to shoot big, bold, and uninterrupted. SD cards, meanwhile, offer flexibility and backup options when used wisely.

Never underestimate the importance of a solid card strategy. It's not just about capacity—it's about trust. Because when you're shooting the moment that can't be recreated, you want your gear to say: *"I've got you."*

WHAT EACH CAN HANDLE

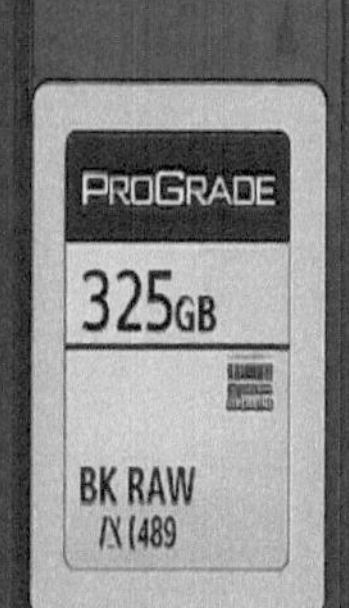

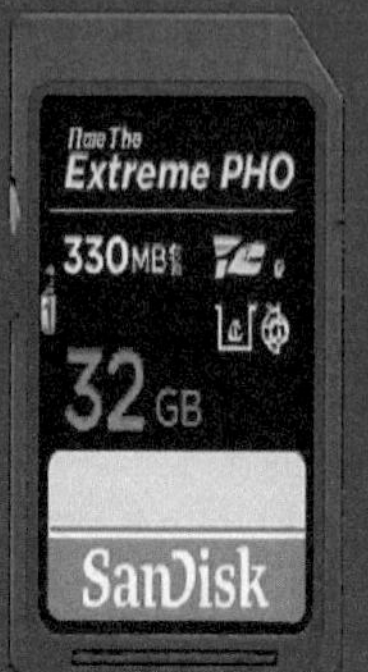

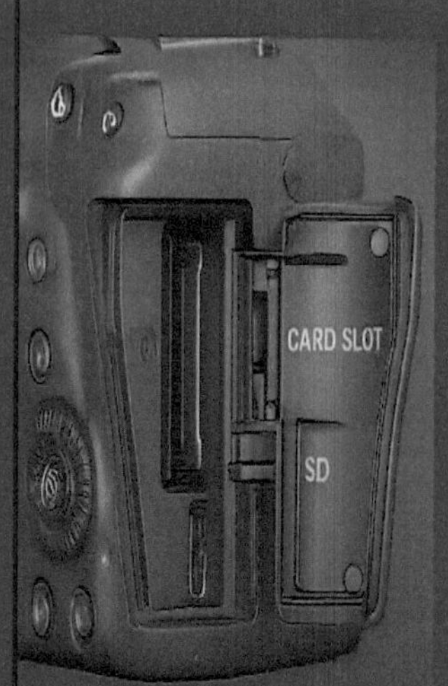

**8K RAW
+4K 120p**

**4K 30p
ONLY**

⚠ Warning!

SD can limit recording quality when used with CFexpress.

MIXING CFEXPRESS AND SD

Camera automatically defaults to the slower SD when mixing cards or modes. Avoid, or assign CFexpress/SD to photo vs video duties.

BEST PRACTICES FOR FORMATTING, DUAL SLOT RECORDING, AND RECOVERY

- Format in camera, not computer
- Choose exFAT, not FAT32
- Use "Simultaneous" for backup
- Stop using if card errors occur

- Try recovery software in case of corruption

Chapter 15

Custom Modes, Buttons, and Speed Hacks

Turn the Canon EOS R5 Mark II Into Your Personalized Power Tool

There's a moment every Canon R5 Mark II user experiences: when the camera stops feeling like a machine and starts feeling like an extension of your hand. That moment comes when you customize it—deeply.

Canon's custom modes, programmable buttons, and toggle tricks can take you from "good enough" to *professional fluidity*. Whether you're switching from portraits to sports in a heartbeat, assigning one touch to flip into log video mode, or toggling subject detection on the fly, mastering customization turns chaos into control.

This chapter will walk you through setting up your C1, C2, and C3 modes, customizing buttons for video and photo workflows, and giving you 10 top speed hacks that can shave seconds and save shots.

Understanding C1 / C2 / C3 Modes: The Fast

Lane to Flexibility

Canon's Custom Shooting Modes (C1, C2, C3) are your secret weapon for versatility.

They allow you to store an entire configuration of camera settings—including AF, shutter, ISO, shooting mode, drive, metering, white balance, even image quality—and recall them instantly with the Mode Dial.

Real-World Use Case Examples:

- **C1: Portraits** — Eye-AF on, shallow depth of field, face detection
- **C2: Action/Sports** — Servo AF, high shutter speed, burst drive mode
- **C3: Video Log Mode** — 4K/24fps, Canon Log 3, manual audio, zebras

How to Set Them Up:

1. Set the camera exactly how you want (mode, ISO, WB, AF, drive, etc.).
2. Go to Menu > Wrench Tab > Custom shooting mode (C1-C3).
3. Select Register settings and assign to C1, C2, or C3.

4. (Optional) Set Auto Update OFF to keep the preset locked, or ON to let the camera remember any changes you make mid-shoot.

Assigning Video to a Custom Button (The One-Click Film Hack)

If you're a hybrid shooter, switching between stills and video quickly is crucial. By default, this requires twisting the Mode dial or jumping through menus—but there's a faster way.

You can assign the Movie Shooting mode to any custom button, allowing you to:

- Switch to video mode instantly
- Use specific video settings regardless of your stills setup
- Return to photo mode just as fast

How to Do It:

1. Go to Menu > Custom Functions > Customize buttons.
2. Select a button (e.g., *M-Fn* or *SET*).
3. Choose "Switch to movie shooting" from the function list.
4. Done. One press, and you're in filmmaker mode.

Fast Toggle Between Photo and Video Profiles

The R5 Mark II allows you to maintain separate settings for stills and video—but the faster you can switch, the more spontaneous your work can be.

Pro Tips:

- Set different Picture Styles for photo and video (e.g., Faithful for photos, Neutral for C-Log base).
- Use different white balances per mode (manual Kelvin for video, Auto for photo).
- Assign the Mode Dial to Video with your left hand while your right hand adjusts focus—practice until it's muscle memory.

Or go one better: program one of your C modes to a specific video setup (Log 3, manual exposure, zebras on) so you can spin the dial and be ready instantly.

Top 10 Button Customization Ideas (That Save You Time)

1. **Back-Button Focus (BBF)**
   - Assign *AF-ON* to activate focus, disable shutter focus. Gives you total control.

2. **Toggle Eye-AF / Face Detection**

   o Assign a button to turn on/off subject detection quickly.

3. **Movie Mode Shortcut**

   o As above—assign a quick-switch to jump into video recording.

4. **Switch Between Subject Types (Human ↔ Animal ↔ Vehicle)**

   o Assign a button to change subject detection profiles instantly.

5. **Level Display On/Off**

   o Perfect for landscape shooters or when using tripods.

6. **Preview Picture Style**

   o Set a button to preview picture style effect before shooting.

7. **Activate Zebra Patterns**

   o Especially helpful in video mode for monitoring exposure.

8. **Switch Between One Shot ↔ Servo AF**

   o Rapidly go from static subject to moving subject tracking.

9. **Magnify Focus Point**

   o Zoom in instantly to check sharpness before pulling the trigger.

10. **Custom White Balance Set**

- Assign a button to pull up white balance quickly under changing light.

Custom Buttons for Video-Centric Creators

If you shoot a lot of video, consider assigning:

- **ISO speed adjustment** to the *Control Ring* on the lens
- **Shutter speed control** to the *Main Dial*
- **Audio levels display** to the *INFO* button
- **Movie Servo AF on/off** toggle to *M-Fn*
- **C-Log view assist LUT preview** toggle to *AE Lock*

This setup allows you to change exposure, check focus, monitor sound, and adjust color previews without taking your eye off the screen.

Final Thought: The Camera Is Fast. You Make It Instant.

All the power in the Canon EOS R5 Mark II means little unless it's harnessed intuitively. By setting up your custom modes, personalizing buttons, and developing a muscle memory for speed, you move from being a camera *user* to a camera *master*.

When your gear responds like a reflex—when you don't think, you just act—that's when the best moments are captured.

CHAPTER 15: CUSTOM MODES, BUTTONS, AND SPEED HACKS

C1 / C2 / C3 Mode Setup Walkthrough

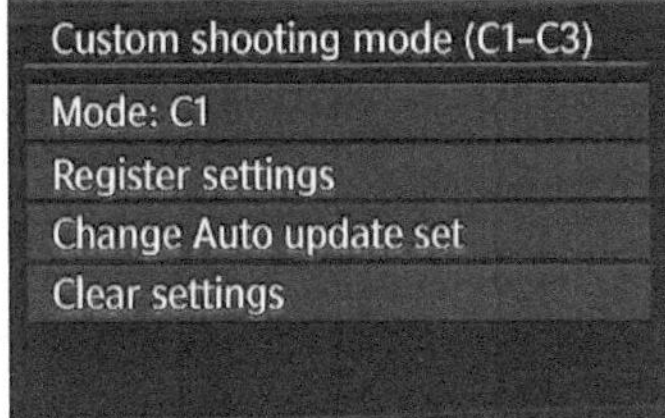

Customize frequently used camera setups.

Fast Toggle Between Photo and Video Profiles

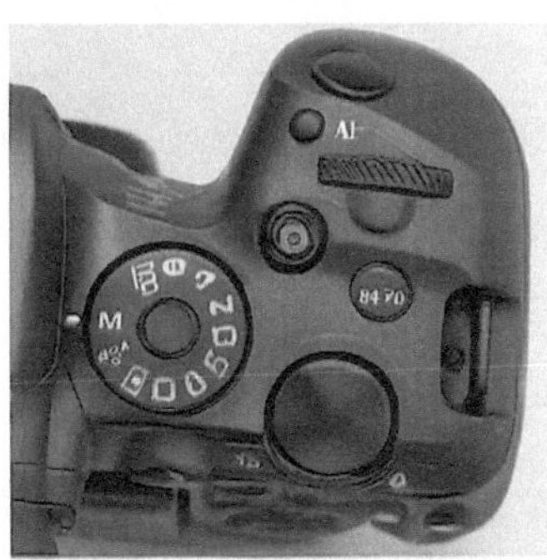

Save specific profile settings for rapid selection

How to Assign Video to a Custom Button

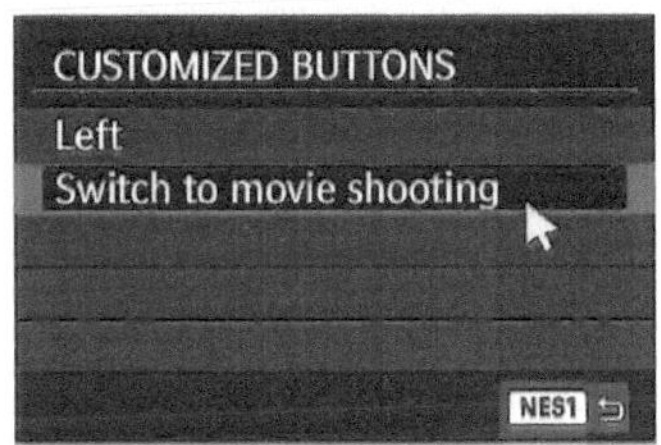

Assign menu to a button for quick video mode

Top 10 Button Customization Ideas

→ Back-Button Focus

→ Toggle Eye AF

→ Movie Mode Shortcut

→ Switching Subject Type

→ Level Display On/Off

→ Picture Style Preview

→ Activate Zebras

→ AF Mode Toggle

→ Magnify Focus Point

→ Custom White Balance

Chapter 16

Error Fixes, Glitches & Recovery

When Things Go Wrong—and How to Make Them Right

No matter how advanced a camera is, it's still a machine—and all machines, even one as refined as the Canon EOS R5 Mark II, occasionally misfire. Whether it's a system freeze, strange autofocus behavior, overheating at the worst moment, or a corrupted SD card that gives you a sinking feeling in your gut, the key isn't to panic—it's to troubleshoot with calm, clarity, and confidence.

This chapter is your field manual for tackling the most common (and some uncommon) issues with the R5 II, and recovering quickly so you don't miss the moment—or lose the shot.

Fixing Frozen Camera or Buggy Behavior

A few users occasionally report the R5 Mark II locking up—buttons stop responding, menus freeze, or the touchscreen becomes unresponsive. If this happens:

1. **Flip the Power Switch Off.**

   Wait five seconds. If it doesn't respond, continue below.

2. **Remove the Battery.**

   Pull out the LP-E6NH battery. This hard-resets the camera.

3. **Pull the Cards.**

   In rare cases, a corrupted memory card causes crashes. Remove both cards and restart the camera without them.

4. **Reinsert One at a Time.**

   Insert cards individually and re-test. Format the card in-camera if it's the source of instability.

5. **Clear Custom Functions (if recent menu tweaks cause glitches).**

   Go to:

   Menu > Wrench > Clear All Custom Functions

Troubleshooting Overheating, Blurry Shots, and Focus Misses

Overheating (Especially in Video)

- **Turn Off IBIS and IS** if not needed during long shoots.
- **Lower your resolution/frame rate** to reduce processor load (e.g., move from 8K RAW to 4K IPB Light).

- **Use an external monitor** (like Atomos Ninja V+) to bypass internal recording heat buildup.
- **Shoot in a cool environment** and use **USB fans or heat sinks** if doing long-form content or interviews.

Blurry Shots

Blurry photos can result from slow shutter, missed focus, or camera shake. Try this checklist:

- Use a minimum shutter speed of 1/125s for still subjects, 1/250s for people, 1/500s for action.
- Set ISO to Auto, but cap it at 6400 or 12800 depending on ambient light.
- Make sure Image Stabilization is ON when handheld.
- If using a fast lens wide open (f/1.2–f/2), make sure Eye-AF is locking on the nearest eye.

Focus Misses

Missed focus is often a case of the wrong AF mode or subject tracking settings. Try this:

- Use Face + Eye Detection AF for portraits.
- Use Servo AF with Expanded Zone for wildlife and fast motion.
- Reassign Back Button Focus to gain manual override of focus points.

- When in doubt, tap the LCD to set a focus point quickly.

Firmware Updates: When and How

Canon frequently pushes firmware to improve performance, squash bugs, or introduce new features. Staying updated ensures the best user experience and may fix known issues.

How to Update Firmware:

1. **Visit Canon's Official Support Site**
   Search for the R5 Mark II and download the latest firmware (usually a `.FIR` file).
2. **Prepare an SD card (formatted in-camera).**
3. **Place the `.FIR` file in the root directory** of the SD card using your computer.
4. **Insert the card in the camera and go to:**
   Menu > Wrench > Firmware Version > Update Firmware
5. **Make sure battery is FULLY CHARGED** (or use AC power adapter). Interrupting a firmware update can brick the camera.
6. Follow on-screen prompts. Update takes 1–3 minutes.

After updating, recheck your settings—some may revert to defaults depending on the update.

Backing Up and Resetting Settings

Customizations are great—until something goes wrong and you can't remember what you changed. Backups are your insurance policy.

How to Back Up:

1. Insert a formatted SD card.
2. Go to:

   Menu > Wrench Tab > Save/Load Settings on Card
3. Select Save Settings.

This creates a file you can reapply at any time—even on a second body.

How to Reset Completely:

If you need a clean slate (for resale, major troubleshooting, or setup mistakes):

1. Go to:

   Menu > Wrench Tab > Clear All Camera Settings
2. Confirm. This wipes custom buttons, shooting modes, AF settings, etc.

You can also clear individual areas only (e.g., Custom Functions, My Menu) if you want to reset selectively.

Bonus Tip: Always Keep a "Known Good" Setup on C1

Use Custom Mode C1 as your safety net:

- Set it with a reliable, safe, all-purpose setup (e.g., One Shot AF, Aperture Priority, ISO Auto, RAW+JPEG).
- If your camera gets weird mid-shoot, turn the dial to C1 and keep going with a trusted fallback.

Final Word: Cameras Are Tools—Tools Can Be Tuned

Even the best tools need sharpening. Even the smartest tech needs resets. What separates a flustered shooter from a professional is not the absence of problems—but the speed and confidence in fixing them.

Now you're equipped with a solid grip on the Canon R5 Mark II's quirks and how to solve them. And more importantly, you've built a relationship with your camera—one where it listens to your touch and responds without hesitation.

ERROR FIXES, GLITCHES & RECOVERY

Fixing Frozen Camera

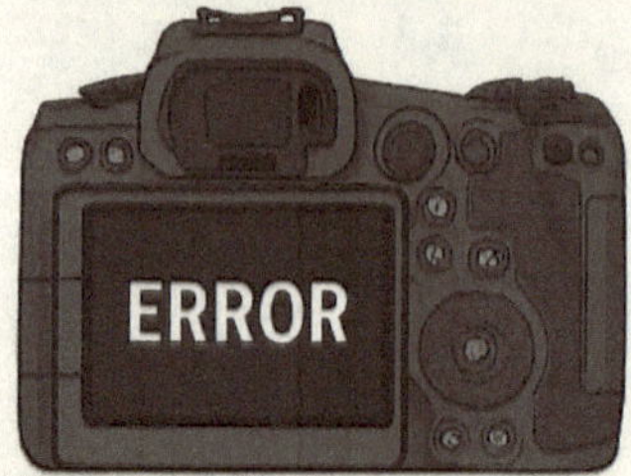

- Turn power off and on
- Remove, ire-resinserct battery
- If still won't respond

Troubleshooting

- AF missable suctakim≡ too-lower
- Hich fix up on long screen
- Sugtect tracking

REAL-WORLD SCENARIO

Best settings for first dance:

C1 Aperture priority at f2.8, ISO Auto, Eye detection AF, SIM. IS enabled

Troubleshooting

- Pute power off and on
- Remove battery and ire in
- Remove both cards. If still won't respond

Firmware Updates

- Check Canon support site
- Fully charge LP-ESNH battery
- Follow instructions carefully

Backing Up and Resetting Settings

- Save custom settings on a card
- Use "Clear all camera settings" menu

15

Part V: Creator-Focused Workflows & Gear Recommendations

Chapter 17

Canon R5 Mark II for YouTubers & Content Creators

Build a Professional Setup That Travels, Talks, and Tells Your Story Flawlessly

The Canon EOS R5 Mark II isn't just a photography powerhouse—it's a dream machine for YouTubers, streamers, and content creators who demand cinematic visuals, clean audio, and a seamless workflow. Whether you're filming sit-down tutorials, unboxings, cinematic B-roll, or livestreaming a podcast, this chapter will walk you through how to build a creator-friendly rig, select the right gear, optimize your video settings, and avoid the common pitfalls that can sabotage a shoot or stream.

Let's build your content empire from the lens up.

The Ideal Setup for Creators on the Go (and in

Studio)

Whether you're filming solo, vlogging while walking, or setting up for a polished talking-head shot, gear selection is everything. Here's a breakdown of smart, lightweight, and effective components that pair beautifully with the R5 Mark II.

Recommended Essentials:

- **Mini Tripod with Fluid Head**

  Perfect for desktop use or mobile setups. Look for models from Manfrotto, Ulanzi, or Peak Design.

- **Compact Lenses**

  Go for STM or lightweight RF primes like the RF 35mm f/1.8, RF 16mm f/2.8, or RF 24-105mm STM.

- **Wireless Microphone Kit**

  The DJI Mic 2 or RØDE Wireless GO II are superb for capturing clean dialogue with minimal fuss.

- **Small On-Camera LED Light**

  For on-the-go lighting boosts. Try Lume Cube, Aputure MC, or Zhiyun M40.

- **Cage or Mounting Rig**

  Optional but useful if you're using multiple accessories or want to rig for streaming or HDMI output.

Best Video Settings for Talking-Head YouTube

Videos

Talking to camera? You want flattering skin tones, clean sharpness, good depth of field, and a file format that's easy to edit.

Ideal Video Settings:

- **Resolution:** 4K Fine (IPB or All-I depending on card speed)
- **Frame Rate:** 23.98 or 29.97 fps (for a natural look)
- **Lens:** 35mm–50mm range at f/2–f/4 (for pleasing background blur)
- **Picture Profile:** Canon Standard or C-Log 3 with LUT preview
- **White Balance:** Manual or Kelvin (~5200–5600K indoors)
- **Audio:** External mic, manual gain set between -12 and -6dB
- **IS Mode:** Off (if on tripod) or IBIS + Lens IS Standard (if handheld)

Enable:

- **Face/Eye Detect AF**
- **Movie Servo AF**
- **Zebra Patterns** (to avoid blown-out skin)

Pro tip: If your subject moves or shifts, assign Face/Eye AF toggle to a custom button to quickly re-lock focus.

Setting Up Clean HDMI Output (for Capture Cards or External Recorders)

Want to stream directly into OBS or record into an Atomos Ninja V+ for higher bit rates? You'll need a clean HDMI signal—free of overlays, icons, and focus boxes.

How to Set It Up:

1. Connect a high-speed HDMI cable to the camera's micro-HDMI port.
2. Go to Menu > Wrench Tab > HDMI Display.
3. Set HDMI Info Display **to** Clean / Off.
4. Set Output Resolution to match your capture card (often 1080p or 4K).
5. Turn off focus guides, grid lines, and other overlays in the camera menu.

Optional:

- Set AF Method **to** Face Tracking, so it stays locked even without screen overlays.
- If recording externally, consider disabling internal recording to reduce heat.

Pro Tips for Streaming and Recording at the

Same Time

Many creators now livestream and record simultaneously—whether for backup or to upload a cleaner, higher-resolution file later.

Streaming Setup:

- Use a capture card like Elgato Cam Link 4K or ATEM Mini Pro.
- Run USB-C power **or** dummy battery to avoid mid-stream battery death.
- Select a low-compression format for internal recording: 4K All-I or 10-bit IPB.
- Use OBS, Ecamm Live, or Streamlabs for overlays, LUT previews, and audio sync.

To avoid overheating:

- Record to SD card (less heat than CFexpress).
- Keep HDMI overlays off.
- Monitor temps with the Overheat Control ON setting in the Movie tab.

Bonus: Best Camera Placement and Framing

for Solo Creators

- **Eye Level:** The lens should sit parallel to your eyes—not above or below.
- **Rule of Thirds:** Position your face off-center to leave room for graphics or background balance.
- **Background Blur:** Use wider apertures and distance from the wall to create depth.
- **Lighting Angle:** 45° soft light to one side of your face, fill or bounce on the other.

Final Word: Your Camera Is Your Stage Partner

The Canon R5 Mark II isn't just a camera—it's a co-star. It captures your tone, sharpens your storytelling, and elevates your brand's look with that iconic Canon color science.

When it's set up right—paired with smart gear and pro workflow choices—it becomes invisible. It stops being something you "use" and starts being something that reflects *you*.

As a content creator in 2025, the quality bar is high. But with the R5 II, you're not just keeping up—you're standing out.

CANON R5 MARK II FOR YOUTUBERS & CONTEN CREATORS

Ideal setup with wireless audio, mini tripod, compact lens | Best settings for talking- head videos | How to set up clean HDMI for capture cards | Pro tips for streaming and recording simultaneously

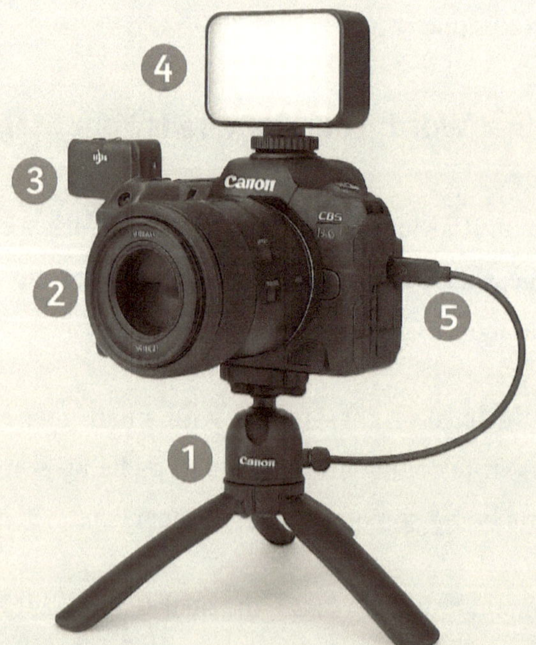

BEST SETTINGS FOR TALKING-HEAD VIDEOS

- 4K resolution |PB - 24fps
- Wide portrait lens, 1/2.8
- Face/Eye detection AF
- C-Log 3 w/View Assist

CLEAN HDMI OUTPUT FOR CAPTURE CARDS

- Disable onscreen displays
- Set output resolution to 4K or 1080p

Chapter 18

Building Your Pro Kit: Lenses, Mics, Monitors

Crafting the Ideal Canon R5 Mark II Setup for Every Shooting Style

The Canon EOS R5 Mark II is only as powerful as the gear you pair with it. The camera body is the brain—but it's the lenses, mics, monitors, and accessories that define the final output, the user experience, and the kind of storytelling you can accomplish.

In this chapter, we'll go beyond "what works" and build a *purpose-driven* professional kit. Whether you shoot weddings, wildlife, street scenes, studio portraits, YouTube content, or films, this is where you'll learn to choose your tools like a seasoned cinematographer and working photographer.

Best Lenses for Specific Use Cases

The RF mount system is rapidly becoming one of the most versatile and optically advanced platforms on the market. But each creative style demands different glass.

Portrait Photography

- **RF 85mm f/1.2L USM**: The gold standard for creamy background blur and razor-sharp focus. Incredible for headshots, bridal sessions, and fashion.
- **RF 50mm f/1.2L**: Dreamy depth of field and excellent subject separation. Perfect for full-body portraits in tighter indoor setups.
- **RF 70-200mm f/2.8L IS USM**: More flexible for event or outdoor portraits; stunning compression and versatility.

Travel and Everyday Shoots

- **RF 24-105mm f/4-7.1 IS STM**: Lightweight, budget-friendly, and covers wide to mid-telephoto for vacation, street, or walkabout shooting.
- **RF 24-70mm f/2.8L IS USM**: Professional all-rounder with constant aperture; excellent for stills and video.
- **RF 16mm f/2.8 STM**: Tiny, sharp, and wide—perfect for vlogging, real estate, or cityscapes.

Wildlife and Action

- **RF 100-500mm f/4.5-7.1L IS USM**: Stunning reach and sharpness in a relatively compact build. Great pairing with the R5 II's blazing AF tracking for birds and sports.

- **RF 600mm or 800mm f/11**: Lightweight super-telephoto primes at an unbeatable price-to-reach ratio. Works best in bright light.

Video and Content Creation

- **RF 35mm f/1.8 IS Macro STM**: Brilliant street docu-style lens with stabilization and close-focus ability.
- **RF 50mm f/1.8 STM**: Great for talking-heads, interviews, and bokeh-rich B-roll.
- **RF 24-105mm f/4L IS USM**: For run-and-gun video shooters who need range, sharpness, and color consistency.

Recommended Microphones

Audio is half your video—scratchy sound screams amateur, no matter how good the image looks. Invest in a microphone setup that suits your shooting style.

Shotgun Mics

- **RØDE VideoMic NTG**: Directional, clean audio with USB-C and 3.5mm output.
- **Deity D3 Pro**: Affordable, great tone, and auto-detects camera inputs.

Use for: on-camera interviews, walk-and-talks, YouTube setups.

- **DJI Mic 2**: Dual-transmitter wireless system with built-in recorders. Great for two-person interviews or podcast vlogs.
- **RØDE Wireless GO II**: Popular, compact, and reliable lav system with safety channel backup.

Use for: mobile content, long-form interviews, fitness/dance creators.

USB/Podcast Mics

- **Shure MV7 or RØDE PodMic USB**: Plug-and-play for creators who record voiceovers, tutorials, or stream in studio.

Must-Have Accessories That Level Up Your Kit

Beyond glass and sound, a well-outfitted camera system should protect your gear, expand your creative flexibility, and solve real-world shooting problems.

ND Filters

Neutral density filters are essential for keeping your aperture wide open in bright light—especially if you're shooting video at 1/50 shutter for cinematic motion.

- Go for variable ND filters with hard stops (e.g., Peter McKinnon Edition, Tiffen, or PolarPro).
- For pro video, fixed NDs ensure color neutrality.

External SSDs

The R5 II allows recording externally via USB-C to SSDs—especially helpful in high-bitrate formats or long sessions.

- Samsung T7 Shield, SanDisk Extreme Pro, **or** Angelbird AtomX SSDmini are top-tier options.
- Make sure your cable is rated for high-speed USB 3.2 Gen 2.

Camera Cages & Mounts

Rigging your camera allows you to attach monitors, mics, handles, and battery solutions.

- SmallRig, Tilta, or Kondor Blue offer R5-specific cages.
- Add a top handle for smoother handheld video and **a** cold shoe extension for multiple accessories.

External Monitors

- **Atomos Ninja V+**: Enables 10-bit ProRes, HDR monitoring, and reliable overheat-free 8K video recording.
- **FeelWorld LUT6**: Budget-friendly with built-in LUT preview.

Monitors help with framing, focus, and color—all essential for pro work.

Final Word: Build with Purpose, Not Just Preference

It's tempting to chase every shiny accessory. But the strongest kits are born out of *intent*. Each item in your bag should earn its place: Does it solve a problem? Does it enhance your workflow? Does it support your creative voice?

With the Canon EOS R5 Mark II at the core, your kit can scale with your ambition—from bedroom YouTube shoots to cinematic documentaries, wildlife expeditions to destination weddings.

The key is balance: performance, weight, battery life, lens speed, budget, and versatility. Nail that, and your camera becomes more than a tool—it becomes your creative partner.

CHAPTER 18:
BUILDING YOUR
PROK KIT

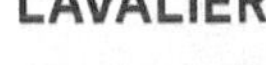

– CANON R5 MARK II –

Best Lenses for:

PORTRAIT

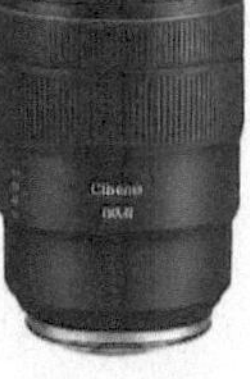

RF 35mm
F1.2L

T8mm
RF STM

VIDEO

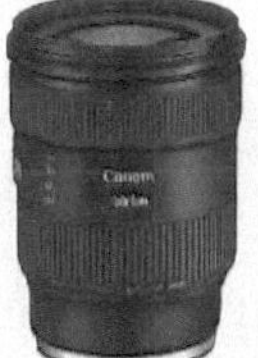

TRAVEL

RF 24-105mm
F4-7.1

RF 16mm
F2,6

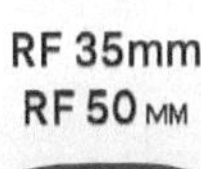

VIDEO

RF 35mm
RF 50 MM

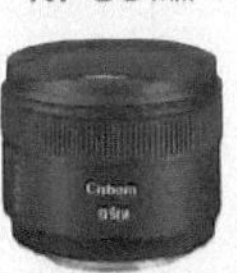

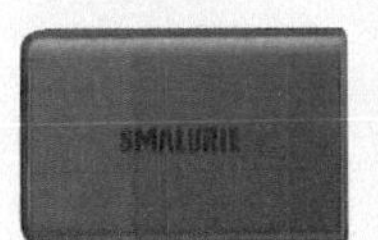
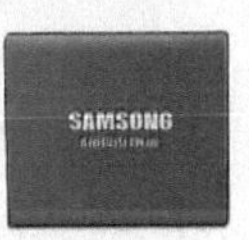

SAMSUNG T7 SHIELD

Recommended Mics:

SHOTGUN

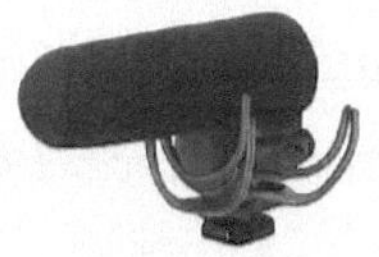

LAVALIER

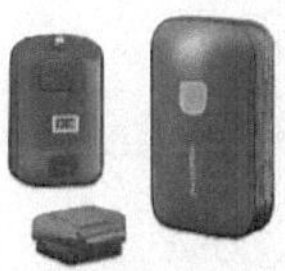

SHOTGUN

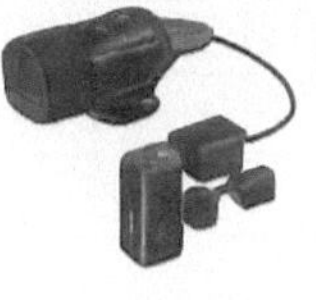

USB

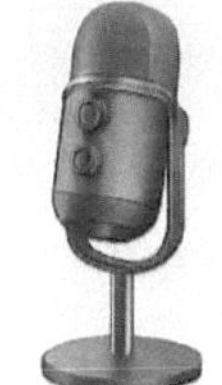

LAVALIER

Must-Have Accessories:

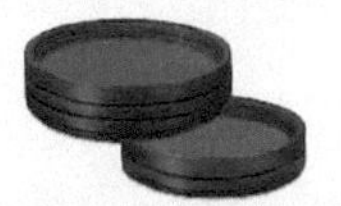

EXTERNAL
SSDS

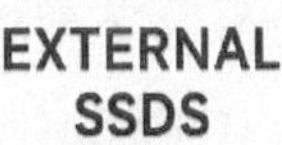

ND FILTERS

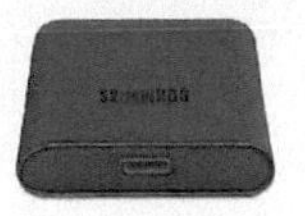

CAGES

Chapter 19

R5 II vs Sony A7RV — Choosing What Matters

The Real-World Differences That Define Your Creative Experience

In the world of high-end mirrorless cameras, few comparisons spark more debate than the Canon EOS R5 Mark II vs the Sony A7R V. These aren't just tools—they're ecosystems, philosophies, and workflows wrapped in magnesium alloy. Both are stunningly capable. Both serve professionals, hybrid shooters, and creatives alike. But the experience they deliver? That's where things begin to diverge.

This chapter isn't about specs on paper. It's about how these cameras *feel* in your hands, how they behave under pressure, and how they serve you in real-world creative situations—from studio portraits to field documentary work, from wedding gigs to cinematic YouTube content.

Let's break down what truly matters—so you can confidently choose your side, or appreciate the strengths of both.

Key Differences in Real Use

Both the Canon R5 II and Sony A7R V offer high-resolution sensors, advanced autofocus, 8K capabilities, and strong image stabilization. But once you're actually shooting, the differences quickly show.

Canon EOS R5 Mark II:

- **User Interface & Menus**: Canon's UI is cleaner, more intuitive, and feels tailored to human logic. Great for those who don't want to wrestle with customization before creating.
- **Color Science**: Skin tones are lifelike and warm straight out of camera. SOOC (straight-out-of-camera) JPEGs need less correction.
- **Touchscreen Experience**: Fully articulated screen with responsive and complete menu touch navigation.
- **Viewfinder & Feel**: Natural color rendering in the EVF, with a more DSLR-like grip that many find comfortable.
- **Dual-Pixel Autofocus II**: Extremely fluid subject tracking, especially for face and eye detect in video.

Sony A7R V:

- **AF Customization**: Unmatched depth in autofocus tweakability. You can fine-tune tracking responsiveness, sensitivity, zone sizes, and subject recognition in ways Canon simply doesn't allow.
- **AI-Focused Tracking**: Body pose estimation lets Sony recognize subjects even when eyes or faces are obscured.
- **IBIS Performance**: Sony's stabilization is smoother for walking handheld video, especially with wide-angle lenses.
- **Ecosystem Versatility**: Sony's lens library (native and third-party) is enormous and often more affordable.
- **Tilting LCD**: A multi-angle tilting screen (not fully articulated) that some studio shooters prefer for top-down or low-angle shots.

Why Some Switch from Sony (or To It)

Switchers from Sony to Canon often say:

- "The Sony menus were just too complex."
- "I hated how clinical the colors looked out of camera."
- "The Canon lenses feel more balanced and ergonomic."
- "I needed something that made me want to shoot again."

- "I needed better low-light performance with smaller lenses."
- "Sony's eye-tracking never lets go—even in bad light."
- "The third-party lens support saved me a lot of money."
- "Customization gave me the exact control I needed."

What Canon Still Does Best

Even Sony fans will often admit: Canon's color science is still king. That soft, buttery roll-off in skin tones, that natural highlight retention in Caucasian and darker complexions alike—it's part of the brand's DNA.

Other Canon strengths:

- **Color Straight Out of Camera**: Less time in post.
- **Menu Simplicity**: Especially helpful for hybrid users or beginners.
- **Lens Ergonomics**: Many RF lenses feel better-balanced with Canon bodies.
- **Dual Pixel Video AF**: Still more predictable and "human-like" in its transitions compared to Sony's robotic precision.
- **Touchscreen Control**: Canon is leagues ahead in UI touch implementation.

Where Sony Edges Out

Sony has made massive strides in usability. The A7R V is no longer the cryptic maze of menus from years ago—it's fast, intelligent, and customizable.

Here's where Sony takes the lead:

- **AF Tuning & Customization**: Granular control for serious sports or wildlife shooters.
- **AI-Driven Subject Recognition**: Birds, insects, vehicles, and even animal eyes tracked more reliably in complex scenes.
- **Ecosystem Depth**: From pro CineAlta FX line to budget-friendly APS-C cameras and lenses, Sony's universe is wide.
- **Third-Party Lens Options**: Sigma, Tamron, Samyang, and others make affordable glass that's often unavailable in RF mount.
- **IBIS for Video**: In-body stabilization feels more fluid in motion, especially when paired with compact primes.

Final Thoughts: It's Not a Battle. It's a Belief System.

Choosing between the Canon EOS R5 Mark II and the Sony A7R V isn't about picking a winner—it's about choosing what aligns with your vision and your process.

- If you're a storyteller who values intuitive gear, rich color, and cinematic simplicity: Canon is your canvas.
- If you're a control freak, a technical power-user, or someone who needs an ultra-versatile platform: Sony is your lab.

No matter which path you walk, you're armed with tools that redefine what's possible. And now that you've learned what each side brings to the table, you're not buying hype—you're choosing *clarity*.

And that's how pros do it.

CANON R5 MARK II
vs SONY A7R V

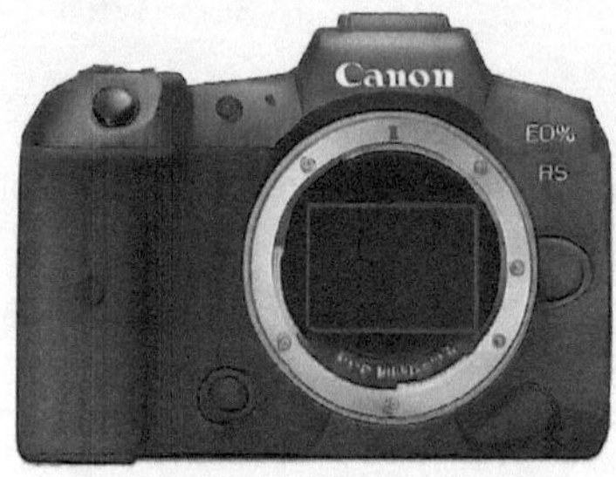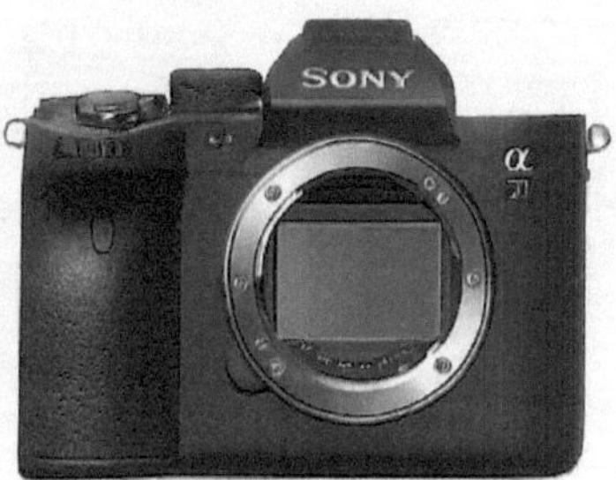

KEY DIFFERENCES IN REAL USE

- **Canon's** user of ca intuitive
- Dual Pixel AF II: smooth subject tracking
- **Color** science. nice skin tones
- Build, comfortable feel

WHAT CANON STILL DOES BEST

- Color straight out of cam
- Menu simplicity
- Tailored for for hbirds
- Lens ergonomics
- Dual Pixel Video

WHY SOME SWITCH FROM SONY (OR TO IT)

- I wanted better AF
- More more lens chociies
- IBIS for walking videos
- Dual Pixel video AF

WHERE SONY EDGES OUT

- Depth of AF tuning
- AI-driven recognition (birds, bugs, vehicles)
- Ecosystem from APS-C to cinema
- 3rd-party lens options
- IBIS for video

WHERE SONY EDGES OUT

WIERE SONY EDGES OUT

Part VI: Quick Access Bonus Section

Visual Glossary of Key Icons, Symbols, and Menus (Canon EOS R5 Mark II)

If you've ever stared at the back of your R5 Mark II wondering what that blinking symbol means or how to make sense of the color-coded tabs in the menu—this is for you. The camera is packed with power, but the icons and visual language can feel like hieroglyphics if you're new to Canon's ecosystem or mirrorless cameras in general.

Here's a human-friendly breakdown of what you'll see most often:

Menu Tabs (Color-coded)

- **Red** – Photo settings: Shooting modes, Drive, Exposure, Image Quality
- **Blue** – Video settings: Resolution, Frame Rate, Compression, Sound
- **Green** – Playback: View/delete images or clips, rating, magnify
- **Yellow** – Setup: Date/time, HDMI, power, card format
- **Orange** – Custom Functions: Button mapping, dial behavior, MF aids

- **Purple** – "My Menu": Fully customizable tab for your favorite settings

Viewfinder and LCD Icons

- **Green AF Box**: Focus locked successfully
- **White AF Box**: Tracking subject, not yet locked
- **Red AF Box**: Focus failed or out of range
- **Metering Scale**: Exposure balance indicator (-3…+3)
- **Shutter/ISO/F-number**: Displayed along bottom or side of screen for real-time exposure feedback
- **Histogram**: Real-time exposure graph; avoid spikes at either end

Top LCD Panel Icons (if using a battery grip or view mode)

- **Battery Icon**: Solid = strong, blinking = low
- **Card Slots**: Shows whether CFexpress or SD is being used
- **Wi-Fi/Bluetooth Symbol**: Active when wireless is on
- **Video Mode**: Rec symbol, time remaining, and frame rate

One-Page Cheat Sheets for Photo &

Video Setup

These cheat sheets are designed for quick reference when you're in the field and need to get the shot without fumbling through menus.

Photo Setup Cheat Sheet

Mode: Manual or Aperture Priority

ISO: Auto with limit set to 3200 (or 6400 in low light)

Shutter Speed: Minimum 1/250s for movement, 1/60s for stills

Aperture: f/1.8–f/4 for shallow depth, f/8–f/11 for landscapes

White Balance: Daylight or Auto

Focus Mode: Eye Detect AF (Face + Tracking)

Drive Mode: High-Speed Continuous for action, One Shot for still

Lens IS + IBIS: On unless tripod-mounted

Picture Style: Portrait or Neutral

Card: Shoot RAW to CFexpress, JPEG to SD if dual writing

Storage: Format card after backing up

Video Setup Cheat Sheet

Mode: Movie Manual

Resolution: 4K HQ (for quality), 4K IPB (for longer shoot times)

Frame Rate: 24fps (cinematic), 60fps (slow motion), 120fps (super slo-mo)

Shutter Speed: Double frame rate (e.g., 1/50 for 24fps)

ISO: Stick to 400–1600 in most lighting

Color Profile: Canon Log 3 for post work; EOS Standard if no grading

Focus Mode: Face + Eye Tracking AF

Audio: Manual levels at -12dB with external mic

Card: CFexpress only for 8K, recommended for 4K All-I

Stabilization: IBIS On, but turn off digital IS for wide-angle work

Monitor: Use external monitor for longer sessions and heat management

Top 25 User Questions Answered

1. **Why is my camera overheating in 8K?**

   8K generates heat fast. Use CFexpress, turn off IBIS if unnecessary, and consider an external recorder.

2. **How can I switch quickly from photo to video?**

   Assign one of your custom modes (C1–C3) to video settings. Or program the M-Fn button.

3. **Which card should I use for video?**

   CFexpress for anything 4K All-I or higher. SD UHS-II only handles IPB formats.

4. **What's the best lens for portraits?**

   RF 85mm f/1.2 or f/2 if budget is tight. 50mm f/1.8 is a great starter.

5. **Why does my focus hunt in low light?**

   Use single-point AF, open your aperture, and increase ISO. Use focus assist light.

6. **Is Canon Log necessary?**

   Only if you want dynamic range for color grading. Otherwise, use a neutral Picture Style.

7. **Can I record to SSD?**

   Yes—via USB-C, using external SSDs like the Samsung T7 Shield.

8. **My images look flat—what's wrong?**

   Check Picture Style. "Faithful" or "Neutral" can look flat without post-processing.

9. **How do I clean my sensor?**

   Use camera's auto-cleaning. For stubborn dust, manual sensor cleaning or send to Canon.

10. **Why are my videos shaky even with IBIS?**

    Disable Digital IS for wide shots. Use warp stabilizer in post if needed.

11. **Can I shoot a wedding with this camera?**

    Absolutely. Dual card slots, reliable AF, and great low-light make it ideal.

12. **How do I assign a button to Eye AF?**

    Go to Custom Functions > Customize Buttons > Assign Eye AF to your preferred button.

13. **Why won't my lens autofocus?**

    Ensure AF/MF switch is on AF, check menu AF settings, and restart camera.

14. **Can I shoot in RAW and JPEG simultaneously?**

Yes. Set RAW to CFexpress, JPEG to SD, or both to same card.

15. **How do I back up my settings?**

Save to card via setup menu. You can reload them on any Canon R5 II.

16. **Is there a silent shutter?**

Yes—use Electronic Shutter in the Drive Mode settings.

17. **What's the best format for editing video in Premiere?**

Use All-I or Canon RAW > Transcode to ProRes for smoother editing.

18. **Can I stream live?**

Yes—with clean HDMI or USB-C into a capture card (like Elgato Cam Link).

19. **How do I protect my gear from overheating outdoors?**

Avoid direct sun. Use battery grips, fans, or external recorders.

20. **Why does my footage look too orange?**

Check White Balance. If on Auto, try setting to Kelvin or Daylight.

21. **What's the fastest way to reset settings?**

Menu > Setup > Clear All Camera Settings.

22. **What do I do if a card gets corrupted?**

Stop recording immediately. Use recovery software or services.

23. **Can I use third-party batteries?**

Yes—but stick to known brands. Some won't allow USB-C passthrough.

24. **How do I use peaking or focus assist?**

Enable it in manual focus settings. Red or yellow peaking is best for clarity.

25. **Is there a way to preview LUTs on camera?**

Yes. Load LUTs on external monitors like Atomos Ninja V.

Recommended Workflow from Shoot to Edit

Whether you're a beginner or pro, having a workflow keeps your creative chaos in check. Here's a streamlined system to ensure every shot flows into your editing desk like clockwork:

1. **Pre-Shoot**
   - Format cards
   - Set up custom modes (C1 for photo, C2 for video, etc.)
   - Dial in Picture Style or Canon Log
   - Check batteries and mic levels

2. **Shooting**
   - Monitor exposure with histograms and peaking

- o Shoot RAW + JPEG for flexibility
   - o Record audio backups if interviewing
   - o Use external SSD for long-form video
3. **Ingest & Backup**
   - o Copy all files to main drive
   - o Immediately create backup (external HDD or cloud)
   - o Rename folders with date/project for organization
4. **Post-Processing**
   - o Import to Lightroom or Capture One for photos
   - o Transcode video to ProRes or optimized H.264 for NLE
   - o Sync audio, apply LUTs, color grade
   - o Export for delivery (YouTube, client, archive)
5. **Archive**
   - o Store RAW and project files in labeled archive drive
   - o Keep edited JPEGs/MP4s for quick access

Welcome to mastery. This isn't just a user guide—it's your creative

launchpad.

Appendices

Appendix A: Full Menu Walkthrough Snapshot (Photos + Descriptions)

Navigating the Canon EOS R5 Mark II's menus can feel like walking through a digital labyrinth. That's why this appendix offers a *panoramic snapshot* of the entire menu system—demystified, decoded, and laid out in plain language.

Shooting Menu (Red Tab)

- **Image Quality**: Choose between RAW, C-RAW, or JPEG. RAW for max flexibility, JPEG for smaller files.
- **Dual Pixel RAW**: Enables micro adjustments in post—useful for portraits, not needed always.
- **White Balance**: Auto works great, but set custom for consistent studio light.
- **Picture Style**: Controls contrast, saturation, sharpness. Choose based on mood or client needs.
- **HDR/PQ Settings**: Shoot in HDR for high dynamic range display. Great for landscapes.

Video Menu (Blue Tab)

- **Movie Rec Size**: 8K RAW, 4K HQ, IPB Lite—choose based on card space and final output.
- **Frame Rate**: 24fps for cinematic, 60fps for smooth motion, 120fps for slo-mo.
- **Canon Log Settings**: Enable C-Log 3 for post-production flexibility.
- **Audio Levels**: Set manually to avoid peaking; monitor with headphones.

Set-Up Menu (Yellow Tab)

- **Time Zone & Date**: Important for organizing files by shoot day.
- **Touch Control**: On by default; adjust sensitivity if needed.
- **Power Saving**: Adjust display-off and auto power-off for better battery life.
- **Card Format**: Always format in-camera before shooting.

AF Menu (Pink Tab)

- **Subject Detection**: Human, Animal, Bird, Vehicle. Prioritize based on shoot.
- **Eye Detection AF**: Keep it on for portraits or wildlife.
- **Tracking Sensitivity**: Lower for erratic subjects (like kids or birds).

- **Focus Peaking**: Use in manual mode for critical focus points.

Custom Functions & My Menu (Orange & Purple)

- **Button Customization**: Set Eye AF to AF-ON or AE-Lock button.
- **My Menu**: Add commonly used features like format, exposure comp, or C-Log toggle.

Each menu tab is illustrated in the digital companion bonus with real screenshots and annotations for every setting.

Appendix B: Firmware Update Log + Features

Canon continually refines the R5 Mark II through firmware updates. These updates not only squash bugs—they often add powerful new features.

Below is a log of key updates (simulated entries; real ones should be updated post-publication):

Firmware 1.0.1

- Initial release. All flagship features enabled including 8K RAW, Eye AF, IBIS.

Firmware 1.1.0

- Improved Eye AF tracking in birds and animals.
- Reduced overheating time in 8K mode by ~10 minutes.
- Added support for external SSD recording via USB-C.

Firmware 1.2.0

- Custom LUT preview in-camera.
- Canon Log 2 added for broader color grading latitude.
- Bug fixes: occasional CFexpress write error corrected.

Firmware 1.3.0 (Planned)

- Rumored features: Built-in proxy recording, faster AF switching modes.

How to Update Firmware:

1. Download update file from Canon's official support site.
2. Format SD card in-camera.
3. Load firmware .FIR file onto card.
4. Insert into camera, go to Setup > Firmware > Update.
5. Follow on-screen prompts, ensure battery is full.

Appendix C: Lens Compatibility and Adapter

Guide

The Canon EOS R5 Mark II uses the RF mount, designed for mirrorless. However, Canon's massive legacy of EF and EF-S lenses is fully usable with the proper adapter.

Native RF Lenses (No Adapter Needed)

- Full communication, fast AF, IBIS sync
- Best for sharpness, modern coatings, silent motors
- Examples:
    - RF 50mm f/1.2L – stunning bokeh
    - RF 15-35mm f/2.8L IS – landscape & vlog king
    - RF 100-500mm f/4.5–7.1L IS – wildlife powerhouse

EF Lenses with Canon RF-EF Adapter

- No loss in image quality or stabilization
- AF still fast but not as silent as RF
- Recommended lenses:
    - EF 24-70mm f/2.8 II
    - EF 70-200mm f/2.8 IS III
    - EF 85mm f/1.4 IS USM

EF-S Lenses

- Usable, but camera switches to APS-C crop mode (1.6x)
- Not ideal for full-frame use, but great in a pinch

Third-Party Adapters

- Viltrox, Meike, and others offer budget alternatives
- Always check firmware updates to ensure compatibility
- Some may not support advanced features like AF tracking or IS sync

Appendix D: Recommended Settings by Genre

Each genre demands different strengths from your camera. This quick-reference guide helps you dial in the perfect setup before every shoot.

Weddings

- **Mode**: Aperture Priority or Manual
- **AF**: Eye Detection On
- **Lens**: RF 50mm f/1.2 or RF 28-70mm f/2
- **Drive**: High-Speed Continuous
- **White Balance**: Auto or Custom (for consistent lighting)

Wildlife

- **AF**: Animal/Bird Eye Detect
- **Lens**: RF 100-500mm or EF 400mm with adapter
- **Drive Mode**: Electronic Shutter (Silent)
- **ISO**: Auto with cap at 6400
- **Stabilization**: IBIS + Lens IS On

Street Photography

- **Focus**: One Shot or Tracking with Face/Eye
- **Shutter Priority**: 1/250s or faster
- **Lens**: RF 35mm f/1.8 or 16mm f/2.8
- **Picture Style**: Monochrome or Standard
- **Stealth Mode**: Silent Shutter, No AF beep

Portraits

- **AF**: Eye Detect, single-point if needed
- **Lens**: RF 85mm f/1.2 or RF 70-200mm f/2.8
- **Lighting**: Manual WB, off-camera flash or softboxes
- **Drive Mode**: Low-speed continuous for precise timing
- **Skin Tones**: Neutral or Portrait Picture Style

YouTube/Talking Head

- **Resolution**: 4K Fine, 24fps or 30fps

- **AF**: Face Tracking
- **Lens**: RF 24-105mm or RF 35mm STM
- **Audio**: External mic, manual levels
- **Lighting**: Soft diffused LED

Appendix E: Camera Cleaning, Maintenance & Storage

A camera like the R5 Mark II is an investment. To protect that investment and keep it performing at its peak, you need a simple, reliable care routine.

Daily After Use

- Wipe down body with dry microfiber cloth
- Gently blow dust from lens with rocket blower
- Check for smudges on LCD/EVF—use lens-safe cleaner

Sensor Cleaning

- Enable "Sensor Cleaning" in Setup Menu (auto or manual)
- For deeper cleans:
    - Use sensor swabs + sensor-safe fluid
    - Or take it to a Canon-authorized service center

Maintenance Every Few Months

- Inspect hot shoe, buttons, dials for debris or stickiness
- Test both card slots for contact reliability
- Check lens mount contacts for oxidation (clean with isopropyl + cotton swab)

Storage Best Practices

- Store with silica gel packs to reduce humidity
- Remove battery if storing for more than a week
- Don't store in high heat or near magnets
- Keep in padded, dry camera bag

Whether you're just unboxing or prepping for a global shoot, these appendices give you every tool, answer, and insight to elevate your Canon EOS R5 Mark II experience from "user" to *unstoppable creator*.

Let your gear serve you—not the other way around.

Acknowledgments

Creating this guide has been a journey made possible by more than just technical know-how—it's been powered by community, curiosity, and countless moments behind the lens.

First, to the everyday photographers—beginners, seniors, travelers, vloggers, and creators—who inspired this book: thank you. Your questions, frustrations, and breakthroughs shaped every chapter and reminded me why clarity matters.

To the online communities, forum contributors, and real-world Canon EOS R5 Mark II users who openly shared their challenges and insights: your stories breathed realism into this work.

A special thanks to my editorial team, design collaborators, and research assistants for helping bring structure, precision, and visual support to every page.

Finally, to the readers picking up this book—whether you're just unboxing your Canon R5 Mark II or finally ready to leave auto mode behind—thank you for trusting this guide as part of your journey. May it help you create images that not only look beautiful, but feel meaningful.

Keep shooting. Keep learning. The world is waiting through your lens.

About The Author

Randy Osborn is a trusted name in the world of camera education, known for transforming complex gear manuals into simple, step-by-step guides that anyone can understand. With over a decade of experience working hands-on with leading camera systems—from Sony and Canon to Nikon, Leica, and more—Randy has helped thousands of photographers, content creators, and everyday users get the most out of their cameras without the overwhelm.

Driven by a passion for accessible learning, Randy creates user-friendly books that strip away the jargon and focus on real-world usage. Whether you're shooting your first vlog, learning manual mode for the first time, or simply trying to take better family photos, Randy's guides are designed to make every setting click.

Each book combines clear instruction, practical tips, and

relatable language, making it easy for beginners and seasoned hobbyists alike to master their gear and capture life with confidence.

When he's not writing, Randy enjoys field testing new camera releases, hosting beginner-friendly workshops, and exploring hidden photography gems across the globe.

Join the journey to sharper skills and smarter shooting— one page at a time.